HISTORY AND
THE HUMANITIES

History and the Humanities

by Hajo Holborn

Introduction by Leonard Krieger

Doubleday & Company, Inc., Garden City, New York
1972

Library of Congress Catalog Card Number 73–186027
Text Copyright © 1972 by Hanna D. H. Gray, Executrix for the Estate
  of Hajo Holborn
Introduction Copyright © 1972 by Doubleday & Company, Inc.
Printed in the United States of America
First Edition

ACKNOWLEDGMENTS

"The Social Basis of the German Reformation" is reprinted by permission of *Church History,* Vol. 5 (1936), pp. 330–39.

"History and the Humanities," "History and the Study of the Classics," "Greek and Modern Concepts of History," "Wilhelm Dilthey and the Critique of Historical Reason" are reprinted by permission of *Journal of the History of Ideas,* Vol. IX, No. 1 (New York, 1948), pp. 65–69; Vol. XIV, No. 1 (New York, 1953), pp. 33–50; Vol. X, No. 1 (New York, 1949), pp. 3–13; Vol. XI, No. 1 (New York, 1950), pp. 93–118.

"Ernst Cassirer" is from The Library of Living Philosophers, *The Philosophy of Ernst Cassirer,* pp. 41–46, now published by The Open Court Publishing Company, LaSalle, Illinois.

"Misfortune and Moral Decisions in German History" is from *German History: Some New German Views,* ed. by Hans Kohn. Copyright © 1955 by Beacon Press.

"Panorama of 21 Civilizations" (a review of Arnold Toynbee's *A Study of History*) is reprinted by permission of *The Saturday Review* (New York, May 31, 1947), pp. 11+. Copyright 1947 The Saturday Review Associates, Inc.

"The History of Ideas" is reprinted by permission of *The American Historical Review,* Vol. LXXIII, No. 3 (February 1968), pp. 683–95.

"The Science of History" is from *The Interpretation of History,* ed. with an introduction by Joseph R. Strayer (Princeton, 1943), pp. 61–83. Copyright 1943 by Princeton University Press.

CONTENTS

INTRODUCTION

PHILOSOPHERS HAVE long preferred the symbol of Descartes' matutinal dialogues to Hegel's nocturnal bird-watching for Minerva's old owl, but to historians wisdom undoubtedly does come in the evening. I speak here of wisdom, not of knowledge. That any historical knowledge is best gleaned after the action of the day is done is a truism applicable to all in the profession. But wisdom about things historical is a special kind of knowledge, operating on a special scale of time and accessible to a special few. Historical wisdom is the mastery over the past which is exercised through the sure sense of what in it belonged inviolably to the men who lived it and what is linked with the ages and belongs also to us. This is a wisdom that can be neither taught nor created. It must grow, in those who look for it, from the gradual accumulation of historical pieces and the expanding awareness of their connections. It must come in the evening of every historiographical age.

Such was the historical wisdom of Hajo Holborn. He had appropriated, in all its breadth and continuity, the cultural tradition of the West that extended as a kaleidoscopic but unbroken field of force back to Socratic Greece, and he had absorbed it concomitant with historiographical tradition, reaching forward cumulatively from Thucydides. So completely and so actively did he make these legacies his that the double vision they bequeathed became his own mode of perception. He saw every human reality stereoptically, bearing a twofold truth: the truth of its meaning—that is, of what its relations with other realities made it; and the truth of its existence—that is, of what it was inimitably in itself. In history, the latter truth must be re-created, but the general truth of any past human deed or being is available to the analytic observer as it never is in the present, precisely because the accumulation of historical knowledge reveals the far-flung net in which all human things are implicated. Because Holborn was a generic Westerner, authentically European by nurture and authentically American by adoption, he conceived his role to be the recapitulation of our culture's past, rooted in Europe, for assumption by the culture's future, adumbrated in America. But though he scoffed at the idea of anyone's retrospective monopoly on truth and put himself in the long line of historians who have reinterpreted the Western past for their own successive generations, his work now appears to confirm the less modest Hegelian notion of history's convergence toward its chosen historians. Certainly we no longer have Holborn's education in all of the many sides of the Western past; and his abiding faith in continuity, both within the past and between the historical past and the present historian of it, is rapidly being displaced by the belief in actual discontinuity, asserting the autonomy of historical quanta both within the past and for the relations of past with present, or by the belief in moral discontinuity, asserting the continuity only of evil and oppression and the consequent ethical necessity of the historian's deliberate break from it. Those of us who hold to a usable past will have to learn of it from historians like Holborn who undertook to translate the total bearing of it into a language which we can still understand.

To write so of the author of the essays that follow is less to praise him than to characterize them. In his last years, even while Holborn was capping the general history he did so well with his magisterial three-volume *History of Modern Germany,* his attention turned ever more to the history of ideas as the most appropriate field for demonstrating the unity of the past and its relevance to the present. He devoted to it his presidential address to the American Historical Association,[1] and he cherished the project of a final book which would assemble a careerful of inquiry, research, and thinking on this subject and would fittingly seal his life's work. He felt that in his lectures and articles over the years he had supplied himself with the essential components of such a book and they are, indeed, so consistently pervaded by his approach to the integrity of history and by his conviction of his mission to fructify the present in terms of it that they would have required comparatively little in the way of revision and addition to put the finishing polish on his testimonial to the spirit of Western civilization.

For there is a definite crystalline quality about these essays. Whether taken in cross section, by the piece, or as an aggregate, their structure is the same. They are bound together by a homogeneity of tone and level, by the complementarity of their themes, and by the over-all integration of the cultural fields they severally occupy.

The even tone that pervades these essays is the stylistic counterpart of the crucial intermediate level on which their substance is steadily pitched. The characteristic Holbornian tone is a blend of notes usually struck as discordances—of sympathetic warmth and critical shrewdness, of narrative description and rational analysis, of participation in the past *sub specie temporis* and of judicious thoughtfulness about long-range effects and developments *sub specie aeternitatis*. The blend, moreover, is an integration rather than a balance of these qualities, a step beyond the equipoise which was featured in the styles of Ranke and Meinecke, the two predecessors who come closest to the kind of historian that Holborn was. Any typical sequence out of the following essays demonstrates what lies behind their homogenized style. Whether we look at, say, the relations of Thucydides and Machiavelli in "Greek and Modern Concepts of History" or

[1] See "The History of Ideas," below.

the political role of Luther and Lutheranism in "Power Politics and Christian Ethics in Early German Protestantism"—
to take two random examples—it is clearly the distinctive
and sophisticated use of historical criticism that modulates
the reconstructed description of the actual past so smoothly
into the corrected analysis of its meaning for the future. For
historical criticism in these essays is a two-sided activity, with
the two sides exhibited in smooth succession. First, criticism
is directed against later historiographical encrustations to re-
produce the original past in its own terms. Then criticism is
turned against the original terms of the past to correct its expectations in terms of how it was actually received by the successors who were developing along the same line of ideas.
Hence the level tone that forms the stylistic link among these
essays is the natural vehicle of an approach which, eschew-
ing the usual variations between individual fact and general
interpretation, sees a single process composed by the series
of double-edged ideas, each referring both to the historically
identifiable persons and groups who inimitably bore it and
to its projected relations with subsequent ideas which took it
into account in its guise of a universal truth. When facts are
ideas, general connections between the facts are not constructs
or even inductions of the historian but are themselves a kind
of fact, to be ascertained by the historian's blend of description and analysis like any other kind of fact.

This leveled language is attuned to an equally uniform level
of the ideas which are the foci of the essays. As all students
of intellectual history know, ideas vary not only with historical time but with social space: at any one time the same
category of ideas takes diverse forms ranging from the logically articulated systems of formal thinkers to the assorted
psychic stock of unreflective doers, and it consequently makes
sense to look for the level of the ideas on which intellectual
historians operate. In this book the level is one of applied or
engaged ideas—that is, of formally articulated ideas in the
hybrid forms they take when they are deliberately accommo-

dated to the requirements of historical, political, and social existence. As the treatment of both Hegel and Marx in "The Philosophy of History of Karl Marx" exemplifies, the characteristic structure of the presentation is to set forth original systems of ideas, illuminated by their political and social conditioning but in themselves independent of such conditioning, not for the purpose of discussing these systems themselves but for the purpose of showing the origins of the ideas that are the foci of discussion—the ideas that are applied to the historical manifold of men's actual life in society. It was, indeed, Holborn's own propensity for this level of ideas that helped him to his brilliant perception of the role of ideas for Marx—that he reprobated only "pure ideas" and that he considered socially engaged ideas to be "the transmission belt" of history.

The kind of intellectual engagement herein manifested may be seen as a distinctive methodological contribution to intellectual history. Two generic currents dominated the genre during the first half of our century, currents that may be labeled the philosophic and the social. The first, associated especially with the German line running from Dilthey to Weber and Meinecke, stressed the autonomy and integrity of ideas and their tensile relations to one another and to existential conditions hypostatized in political power. The second, subdivided into a French mode of defining indefinite and a-rational collective mentalities through social rationalization, a Russian mode of attaching ideas to a specific social group of "intelligentsia," and an American mode of viewing ideas as instruments of reform, stressed the social formation of ideas to the neglect or depreciation of the internal rational coherence cherished by an elite of thinkers. In the essays composing this volume ideas retain their integrity and are invested, as such, in society. Holborn's openness to the daily social matrix of all human productions enabled him to go beyond the tensions which his German predecessors raised to predominance in the history of ideas when they confronted ideas with reality in the form of antipodal political power, but he retained enough of his faith in the force of ideas to maintain his understanding of their continued integrity in the midst of their social commitment. Holborn's understanding of the political, social, and generational conditioning of "Jacob Burckhardt as Historical Thinker," like his breath-taking perception, in "The Social Basis of the German Reformation," of the German clergy's mediatory role between religion and society would hardly have been possible from another approach. And the definition of the intellectual historian's task in general as the pursuit of recognizable ideas in their social employments is precisely the point of the climactic address on "The History of Ideas."

This instance is but one of several which reveal the thematic pattern of the book: a theme that is implied by historical example in one essay is explicated by historiographical exposition in another. There are at least three such themes, weaving their way through the book, signifying their presence in the reappearances of nodal historical figures (Thucydides, Hegel, Ranke, Dilthey), linking the discrete chapters in a common set of concerns, and surfacing in certain key essays to become the objects of direct confrontation. Together they constitute the over-all thesis of the work.

First, there is the role of classical culture—particularly its ancient Greek branch—in modern history. The striking overt aspects of the ancient classics' role in these should not obscure what is not so obvious but is at least of equal importance in it. The essay "Introducing Thucydides" and the application of him to "Greek and Modern Concepts of History" in particular make the point that is made in general through the illuminating survey of the changing approaches to the ancient heritage in "History and the Study of the Classics"—to wit, that the classics are still relevant to us not only because they originated our own culture and have remained astonishingly prominent in the thinking of its recent authoritative figures but because the attitude toward the classics represents a main line of continuity through the successive stages of our culture and has become a common measure for our self-assessment. But even this aperçu, revealing as it is, is not yet the ultimate role of the classics. What this ultimate role is can best be seen if the specific essays on the classics are interpreted in light of the chronologically earlier paper on "History and the Humanities," for here it becomes clear that the humanities, and by extension the classical studies in which they have always been rooted, serve the historian as avenues through which he can expand his results into general truths. From this final point of view Holborn's emphatic connection of the study of classics to the study of history serves not only to demonstrate cultural continuity in Western history but to require a corresponding universal outlook in Western historians. Hence the rare appreciation, by a practicing historian like Holborn, of Arnold Toynbee's vast range over "the world of universal history" (in the "Panorama of 21 Civilizations"); and hence too the rare insight by a practicing historian that Toynbee's historiographical problem is not that he is too philosophical but that he is not philosophical enough.

The second running theme in this book is the definition of history as a science. The obvious focus of "The Science of History," it keeps rising as well in the considerations of Marx, Burckhardt, Dilthey, Toynbee, and the classical Greeks. The tendency of these discussions is to show that the study of history both is and should be scientific without being natural-scientific—to show, that is, how the study of history has been, at its best, scientific in its own way. The materials of the argument are drawn preferably from Thucydides and Ranke —the two protagonists of "The Science of History"—and the recurrent references to them are associated with their crucial roles in the construction of the historical discipline as an autonomous science, at once related to and distinct from the other, more prestigious sciences of nature and life which have confused the term by vesting it with their special connotations. In these essays we see, in the paradigmatic cases of

Thucydides and Ranke, how historians applied to their sources critical methods similar to those of the other sciences for the observation and verification of their data, and how they also worked out—to account for the data—the explanatory general truths that all scientists worthy of the title must work out but now in ways different from the generalizations of the natural and life scientists. Holborn's recognition that the scientific ethos requires general and rational as well as particular and empirical truths but that it also comports with several kinds of general and rational truths gave him an unerring insight into the remote historians who felt for a scientifically true history and especially into the great historians of the nineteenth century who strove for a scientific general history of man, and these insights keep striking related notes on a common crucial theme of history as a disciplined study.

The third theme follows from the other two, and indeed it dominates the conclusions of the essays devoted to them. This theme stipulates the function of history to be the understanding of human nature as a totality and its consequent service as the basis of moral action. History is particularly suited for this because it dies when it becomes specialized and loses its sense for the whole and for its mission as a living force ("History and the Study of the Classics"); because it is distorted and becomes an instrument of oppression without "the recognition of the unity of life" ("Misfortune and Moral Decisions in German History"); and above all because it is the one discipline which can fulfill the scientific criteria of objectivity for its general truths only by appropriating the humanities for their contents ("The Science of History"). In short, the "that" in historical generalization is scientific; the "what" is humanistic; the "why" is moral.

Over and above the tone of the language, the level of the ideas, and the subject matter of the themes, there is a final unity which underscores the integral and distinctive contribution of these essays to the study of history. Intellectual history, historiography, and the philosophy of history are usually regarded as separate genres. The first is concerned with ideas as events in the historical process, the second is concerned with the methods, present and past, by which historians ascertain and interpret historical events, and the third is concerned—in the rare instances that historians permit it to be validly concerned at all—with the relationship of historical events and methods to nonhistorical realities and methods which are deemed fundamental by men who are called philosophers for deeming them so. But no such scholastic separation of fields can be found in this book. The overt reason is Holborn's predilection for figures and problems which lie at the intersections of the fields: the philosophers on whom he dwells—Hegel, Marx, Dilthey, Cassirer—were also historians (Hegel most doubtfully, but Holborn is also most doubtful about Hegel); the favored historians—Thucydides, Ranke, Burckhardt—were exceptionally philosophical for historians; and problems like the classical legacy or the social and political impact of the Reformation faced two ways by their very definition as the historical destiny of an insulated set of ideas and doctrines. But behind the versatility of these chosen cases there is a more important reason for the merger of the genres, and it is one, indeed, that helps to account for the choice of these cases. The key is in the opening sentence of the "Greek and Modern Concepts of History": "Only in the Hellenic and Western civilization did historical thought acquire a truly fundamental role for the whole structure of culture." Since history, in the sense of historical-mindedness, was built into the very fiber of Western thinking no sharp line can be drawn between the history of Western ideas and the history of history, which is a charter member in the society of Western ideas; nor can a sharp line be drawn between the methods of acquiring historical knowledge and the epistemological principles of acquiring any kind of knowledge; nor can a sharp line be drawn between the humane values which moral philosophers derive from Western culture and the historical truths which historians derive from that same culture.

What Hajo Holborn has left us, then, is an interlocking set of perspectives on the intellectual sinews of our past. We shall not see so long a view and so composed a vision soon again.

Leonard Krieger

HISTORY AND THE
STUDY OF THE CLASSICS*

I

GREEK, ROMAN, AND CHRISTIAN ideas are the main spiritual
sources of Western civilization. Since Augustine, Christian
ideals have dominated Western life. But Christianity might
not have been able to conquer the West if it had not found in
Greek philosophy the intellectual forms to translate its religious faith into doctrines which protected Christian religion
from dissolving into mere sentiment. The Christian faith,
though beyond human reason, could be defended by reasonable argument and thereby much more effectively taught.
Rome on her part endowed the West with her unique capacity
for organizing the world in a lawful order.

The three elements were united in medieval civilization.
Christian and Greco-Roman motives, however, were not
easily harmonized and the Middle Ages were characterized
not only by movements reasserting a more exclusive Christian ideal of life but also by intellectual movements aiming at
the fuller absorption of classic thinking. There was a sequence of reformations and renascences in the Middle Ages.
Of course, this process could not be adequately understood if
it were conceived of as a merely ideological process and even

* This paper was originally presented to the Conference on the Goals
of Scholarship in the Classics, which met under the auspices of the Depart-
ment of Classics, Princeton University on September 8–9, 1949.

less if construed in a Hegelian fashion with Greco-Roman and Christian ideas forming a clear-cut thesis and antithesis in the dialectical progress of history.

St. Thomas used the new Aristotle, as he became known in the twelfth century, for a sharper and profounder definition of Christian teaching, while on the other hand the early Italian Renaissance found a new access to antiquity through Augustine. Petrarch sensed in Augustine's psychological analysis of the individual, his love of nature, and, most of all, his power of literary self-expression, the great world of antiquity. He turned away from the scholastic interpretation of life and searched for classic beauty and wisdom. Luther also found in Augustine an ally in his fight against the schoolmen, but he went from Augustine not to classic antiquity but to St. Paul and the gospels. Christian and Greco-Roman motives remain interwoven even in the late Middle Ages and early modern times. But the scope of classical knowledge had already been growing since the high Middle Ages, and beginning with the Renaissance and Reformation the polarity of Christian and ancient ideas was becoming a more consciously experienced problem.

The Italian Renaissance disregarded the Christian way of life more radically than had any movement of the previous thousand years. The Italians in the city-states of this epoch found in classical literature and art the guides for the conduct and aspirations of their own secularized life. Thus the studies of antiquity became the true education of those who wanted to realize the highest human potentialities. Leonardo Bruni could, therefore, simply call them in 1401 the *studia humanitatis*. Erasmus was wont to term them, a century later, *litterae humanae* or *studia humaniora*.[1] The revived Ciceronian ideal of *humanitas* comprised a wide range of ethical and aesthetic values. Between Machiavelli's earthly ideal of *virtù*, which is probably best rendered in English as "manliness," and the concept of *humanitas* of Marsiglio Ficino, which considers it the outflow of *divinitas,* there seems to be a wide distance. R. Pfeiffer has rightly pointed out[2] that to practically all the Italian humanists *humanitas* was a lost Roman heritage that had to be regained. *Romanitas* and *humanitas* were identical, and *latinitas,* i.e., the classic Latin language, was the medium by which the Roman ideal could be revived. Erasmus gave the ideal of *humanitas* a more universal meaning by removing the national Italian coloring and by strengthening its ethical foundation.

Whatever forms, however, the *humanitas* ideal took in the next three centuries, antiquity became to its devotees the "classic" world from which the highest norms of human life could be derived. By the emulation of the classics humanity could be regenerated and could recapture the creative power that had been lost in the dark *mediae aetates* which separated the present from the golden age. In this approach, everything ancient was naturally significant and the quantitative expansion of the factual knowledge concerning antiquity a noble pursuit. The vast volumes crowded with philological detail without wisdom were justified by this classicist belief. But more was implied. It became the task of the student of the classics to offer the sources of that venerable world in their genuine and authentic form. Here the beginnings of the growth of modern critical methods can be discerned. Theology and jurisprudence had similar needs for the authentication of their sources. Protestant theology had to prove that the Holy Scripture was really, as Luther and Calvin had maintained, "self-explanatory" and that no ecclesiastical authority was called for to dictate the proper methods of exegesis.[3] Catholic theology not only opposed this view; it also endeavored to demonstrate the unbroken and undistorted Christian tradition of the Catholic Church. The jurists were concerned with the conflicts of customary and classic Roman law which the new national monarchies on the Continent used to establish their sovereignties.

It is easy to criticize fifteenth- to eighteenth-century humanism for the limitations of its historical sense. Originally it followed the scholastic pattern very closely by merely substituting classic for Christian authorities. A thousand years of the history of Western civilization were simply labeled as an aberration of the human race. But before reappraising this often stated criticism it is important to emphasize that the classic world was more present and a deeper source of the values of life than it was in the nineteenth and twentieth centuries. The faith that the classic ideal could be revived by emulation may have been largely illusory, as historical results seem to prove, but the modesty displayed by, let us say, seventeenth-century culture in its recognition of the superiority of the classic world was by no means a sign of supineness but of confident and disciplined strength. This generation was willing to learn first in order to be able to build its own house with circumspection.

These centuries had, indeed, much to learn from antiquity not only in terms of the formal principles of education but also in massive knowledge. Leaving aside the very difficult and controversial problem of whether or not the early Italian Renaissance meant an advance or retrogression in scientific research, there can be no question that the progress of science in all its fields: mathematics, physics, chemistry and medicine from the sixteenth to the eighteenth century would have been neither so rapid nor so effective without the new study of the classics. And the same is true of literature and art as well as of philosophy, psychology, political science, military science, jurisprudence, and history. The revival of Greek and Roman science was at the same time the expression of the conditions and aims of the new society that had come into being in the West and this society displayed a novel capacity to master reality. The development of modern technology and the study of economics, something unknown in Greece, illustrate this point most clearly. Yet in most of its intellectual efforts, antiquity served as a quarry from which could be mined not only pieces of marble to embellish the structure of early modern culture, but solid rocks for its anchorage as well.

II

The classicist humanism of the early modern age originated in a deep longing for a new society and a new individual. The countries which after the Italian Renaissance were foremost in developing the new secular organization of Western civilization, France, the Netherlands, and England, became also the leaders of the humanist movement. Under the influence of Jacob Burckhardt, all modern humanism has been understood one-sidedly as the unfolding of modern individualism and too little attention has been given to the significance of humanism in social history. While it is true that the individual broke away from transcendental authority and asserted his natural capacity for self-improvement, the individual still remained conscious of his membership in a group and in the national community, a group of groups. Humanism fostered a spirit of "liberality," but used the classics to find rules of conduct for certain social types, like the courtier, the nobleman of the robe, the officer, the patrician, the gentleman, etc. And humanism also was one of the driving forces in early modern nationalism.

We can venture to say that the trend toward the establishment of new social conventions in all fields of intellectual, ethical and aesthetic endeavor led to an emphasis on those aspects of antiquity which taught regular and balanced forms. But the humanists and classicists were also eager to advance the general welfare of their national communities, of which they felt themselves to be the true intellectual leaders. The immediate usefulness of classical learning in public affairs strongly buttressed the position of humanism. Napoleon was still conscious of this role of classicism, which he tried to revitalize in order to unify the French society that had been shaken to its foundations by the Revolution.

By the end of the eighteenth century, however, the direct usefulness of classical learning was rapidly waning. Modern science and technology were moving with great strides toward achievements which dwarfed any comparable accomplishment of the ancients. Moreover, the national civilizations had come of age. Perrault's *Querelle des anciens et des modernes* (1688 ff.), raising the problem of whether the modern world had not already outdistanced ancient culture, was the literary prologue to the outward decline of classicist humanism. French humanists began to write French instead of Latin and even to propagate French as the new classical language. But their success, though not inconsiderable, was short-lived. Sooner or later the modern national languages triumphed over French, but at the same time over Latin.

A new and radically different attitude to the classic world was born in the second half of the eighteenth century. Only the major contributing forces can be briefly sketched here. The eighteenth century, so often accused of having been without historical sense, was on the contrary the century that laid the foundation for the modern concept of history.[4] Now, history was finally and completely secularized. History was the history of man. This Thucydides had already taught, but the eighteenth-century thinkers did not merely return to Thucydides. They continued to wrestle with certain fundamental problems which Christianity had raised.

History had to be understood as universal history, and now, not only did the relationship of Israelite-Christian and Greco-Roman history have to be explored, but the civilizations of Asia and the Middle East, which became better known in this period, had also to be fitted into a unified pattern of universal history. Vico, with greater philosophical depth than Polybius, attempted to construe universal history in a cyclical fashion, and the rise and fall of civilizations was a vexing problem to most eighteenth-century thinkers and historians. But in general a teleological construction prevailed, and the idea of progress has continued to exercise a predominant influence upon nineteenth- and even twentieth-century thought.

The new problems brought to the fore by eighteenth-century speculation called for a new scholarly treatment of the classics. As long as the classics were the unchallenged treasury of wisdom and practical knowledge and as long as it was believed, in analogy to Aristotle's definition of art as the imitation of nature, that through the emulation of the ancients access to the good life could be gained, the men who collected philological information wore a halo. Now the philologists were taken to task for assembling the dead material of the past instead of concentrating upon the study of those living matters which could help to shed light upon the new historical problems. Impatiently, the philosophers not only ridiculed the humanists who turned up so much dust that they could no longer see the sun, but they also threw away most of the critical methods which had come into existence. They were replaced either by the philosophical abstractions or by the common-sense judgments of a generation which was exceptionally convinced of its own rectitude.

Needless to say, Gibbon cannot be accused of neglecting the critical methods of the scholarship of his age, and he proved his genius also by the literary form of his presentation, which was learned from the great literature of the period. In the general interpretation of his historical subject he represented, however, the ideas of his time. The hostile disregard of critical method found its strongest expression in Voltaire's *Philosophie de l'histoire*. His "philosophy of history" meant not much more than history as far as it was worthwhile knowing from the point of view of the philosophy of the Enlightenment, and the book displayed glaringly the advances and shortcomings of eighteenth-century history. Erasmus had once written the *Enchiridion Militis Christiani*, the humanist pro-

gram of his *philosophia Christi,* on the insistence of the wife
of a French knight. Voltaire wrote his *Philosophie de l'histoire*
for the Marquise du Châtelet to show that history was not the
monopoly of bald professional men but the concern of every
human individual aiming at a personal education. History
thereby received a new significance and urgency.

It has been often said, and not without good reason, that the
eighteenth-century interpretation of man and human civilization was severely handicapped by its rationalistic beliefs and
utilitarian principles. In particular the eighteenth-century attempts to understand the social process by analogy to the
processes of nature—with individuals forming the atoms of
social operations—have been cited again and again to prove
this judgment. There is a great deal of truth in this criticism,
but it should not be overlooked that the eighteenth-century
philosophers also took the decisive steps away from an exclusively atomistic and rationalistic understanding of civilizations. Political history was only a part of the growth of
civilizations. The state, law, religion, arts, sciences, and philosophy were expressions of a deeper unity which constituted
the true riddle of history to be deciphered. And after exhaust-
ing rationalistic and naturalistic explanations, the eighteenth-
century thinkers were led to propose terms like *moeurs, esprit
des lois, esprit des nations,* or "spirit of the age," concepts
which went far beyond a mere rationalistic interpretation of
history.

But with Rousseau the eighteenth century left the old rationalism altogether. He questioned, for the first time, the
value of history for the ethics of the individual. Man was created a pure and good being, but had degenerated through
civilization. The increase of knowledge and the new artificial
manners had suppressed the true sentiment of man. The invention of property brought on the division of labor and the
separation of classes, which awakened evil passions and made
the human intellect the serf of egotistical ambitions. The real
potentialities of man had not been realized in past history.

Rousseau was convinced that man was endowed with a natural perfectibility and, if he started his historical development afresh, he could avoid deformation by a barbarous intellectual culture and inhuman social conditions. A new political constitution and a new educational system were required to make it possible for the individual to unfold his natural capacities freely and completely.

In Rousseau's opinion the real force of life lay in the natural good qualities of man, which could produce a happy world, if their élan was not crippled or misdirected into artificial channels. Social rules and intellectual conventions were bound to stifle the individual's spontaneous creative power, which rested not only in his reason, but in his feeling and volition as well. The genius of man was to be found in the harmony of these qualities, and such a man could build the world according to his image. Rousseau's modern individualism sounded the death knell of classicist humanism. The latter's theory of learning through emulating the ideal forms revealed in classical history could not stand up against Rousseau's theory of education in which everything was to be the free production of the individual himself.

Rousseau's philosophy of man, in contrast to his political philosophy, found its greatest echo in Germany. The picture of Rousseau was the only decoration in Kant's study; Kant asserted the creative power of man's pure and practical reason and admitted the "genius" in his aesthetics. But even more enthusiastic was the cult of the human genius in the literary movement known as *"Sturm und Drang."* Among the men who inspired this movement was Herder. Herder, however, did not believe, as Rousseau did, that man had to forget history in order to regain his natural heritage. On the contrary, the natural capacity of man had unfolded in history. History was the realization of *humanitas,* and in the idea of *humanitas* was to be found the key for an understanding of the manifold expressions of historical life. Through the unifying understanding of life as the incarnation of *humanitas* men will be able to reach even greater heights of self-realization.

III

Herder's view of history, invigorated by Rousseau's doctrine of the innate qualities of the individual, was the proem to the modern approach to history and to a humanism that was no longer based exclusively on the Greco-Roman antiquity but on world literature and world history. Still there arose simultaneously in Germany from similar sources a new classicism which found its great artistic expression in Lessing, Goethe, Schiller, and Hölderlin, and its scholarly expression in J. J. Winckelmann, C. G. Heyne, F. A. Wolf, G. Hermann, W. von Humboldt, B. G. Niebuhr, A. Boeckh, F. G. Welcker, and others. But German classical scholarship expanded its scope and methods continually, finally bursting the limits of the classics, and turning into history. The progress of contemporary philosophical thought from Kant to Fichte, Hegel, and Schleiermacher ran in a parallel direction. The old Goethe, too, proceeded from classicism to a broader idea of humanism when he attempted, for example, to absorb the wisdom of the Orient.

German neoclassicism of the late eighteenth and early nineteenth centuries shifted the interest from Rome to Greece. The Greeks seemed to provide the model for a solution of the conflict between human freedom and spontaneity on the one side and the necessity imposed by civilization on the other. It should be noted that German neoclassicism as a rule did not demand both a new education and a new constitution to cure the ills of civilization, but only a new education. There were exceptions to this rule. It must suffice to mention here the political philosophy and activity of Wilhelm von Humboldt, though a good many other general reservations should be made with respect to the early nineteenth century. But from the outset the Germans placed the emphasis upon the education of the individual.

German neoclassicism found in the Greeks the ideal of human perfection because Greek art and literature was the spontaneous or—in Schiller's terminology—"naïve" creation of a people which had for a long time, from Homer to Sophocles and perhaps to Aristotle, preserved the natural unity of human capacities that was the highest state of man. It was objectively expressed in what Winckelmann called "the noble simplicity and serene greatness" of Hellas. Thus Rousseau's contention that the natural man was the ideal man was harmonized with Herder's position that man's natural development could take place in history. As the Greeks had maintained their pure *humanitas* in the midst of their civilization, so we could take them as guides to restore the totality of human capacities which was threatened by our own civilization. "All human ailments are healed by pure *humanitas*," said Goethe's Iphigenia. Schiller taught that civilization closes the wounds it inflicts on men. A one-sided intellectual civilization would deface man, but a full culture, which would have to include in addition to reason ethical will power and aesthetic sense, would restore the totality of human nature and produce a higher state of civilization. In German neoclassicism the sense of form and beauty that seemed to hold the mean between the formless desires of man and the fixed rules of reason was the force that guaranteed the totality of human nature. The artistic genius became the ideal individual.

Without probing deeper into the character and range of German neoclassicism, it is immediately clear that it afforded new and profounder insights into the process of history and the nature of historical civilizations. Historical interest was now attracted not only by the late stages of civilizations but rather by their early creative moments when human nature was beginning to unfold its historical forms. Moreover, history was no longer the work of individuals moved by utilitarian ends. It was particularly important that classic scholarship developed methods to cope with the objective forms of civilization. Language had formerly been considered either a gift of God or, by the philosophy of reason, an invention of man. Rousseau already conceived of language as a process in which humanity learned to take charge of its human possibilities. Herder, W. von Humboldt, F. Bopp and others could go on from there to build modern linguistics. Winckelmann was the first to describe the history of Greek art as the expression of the growing national character of a people. Outside of some attempts in post-Aristotelian Greece the history of art before him had been practically identical with the history of artists of the Vasari *Lives* pattern.

The recognition of the objective forms of civilizations, like language and literature, the arts, sciences, philosophy, law, the state, the economy, inevitably led beyond the confines of a single civilization or, as we may also say, beyond classicism. For each of the objective forms of civilization invited not only individual but also comparative study. The study of the classics became the study of human civilization in general.

But before this happened classical scholarship made great advances in its capacity to reconstruct the past. The major individual step in this direction was taken by Barthold Georg Niebuhr. In many respects his personality does not fit into the historical scheme we have presented of the rise in Germany of the new classical learning and the new history. He was not too profoundly affected intellectually by the new literary and philosophical movements but had his personal roots in the preceding period. It was politics more than philosophy that led him to the study of history. He grew up in the agrarian community of North Friesland, which could look back upon an unbroken tradition of social life older than that of the English constitution. The French Revolution imperiled the stability of the historic customs and in fact of any social order. As an eminent member of Baron Stein's group of Prussian reformers Niebuhr could deal with the reform of an absolutistic monarchy and the fight against Napoleon. But at the same time he followed the problem of social and political constitutions into the past.

As a scholar he had learned from the great Dutch philology of Scaliger and from F. A. Wolf's textual criticism and program of an encyclopedic study of antiquity. He was also a sincere admirer of Gibbon, whose use of original sources impressed him. But what Niebuhr accomplished surpassed all his predecessors had done. Louis de Beaufort had already shown, more than half a century before, that the ancient literary sources of the first five centuries of Roman history were often contradictory and to a large extent not grounded on primary evidence. That was a new achievement in the critical treatment of the ancient authors still worshipped as infallible authorities. Just four years before Beaufort's *Dissertation sur l'incertitude des cinq premiers siècles de l'histoire Romaine* was published in 1738, Montesquieu in his *Considérations sur la grandeur et la décadence des Romains* had used Livy with absolute faith. But Beaufort's criticism of Livy and Polybius was literary, and he was satisfied with showing the discrepancies of the written sources and beyond this making some suggestions with regard to the growth of the literary tradition of early Roman history.

Niebuhr agreed that it was the first task of historical criticism to study the genesis of the historical sources going back from the later towards the older and original documents or monuments. The destruction of myth, legend, and forgery must take place in the course of this examination of the sources. But this operation is only preparatory to the "creative criticism" which aims at the reconstruction of lost information and most of all at the establishment of a new unity of historical events and conditions. This critically achieved view of the past as an organic unity is the ultimate goal of historical scholarship, which thereby surpasses the knowledge of the historical actors themselves. Niebuhr claimed that if an ancient Roman were to come to life again he would testify under oath to the truth of Niebuhr's history. We can actually say that Niebuhr understood Roman history better than the Romans themselves.

Niebuhr used in his work freely, and no doubt too freely, methods of analogy with other civilizations. The agrarian life of his own Friesland enabled him to revive the peasant state that Rome had been in her early period. Niebuhr would not have been able to interpret the transformation of the agrarian into a city civilization, upon which the growth of the Roman Empire depended. But whatever mistakes resulted from his liberal use of analogy and an overflowing imagination, they did not affect the hard core of his work, which was the result of a complete mastery of philological criticism made productive by the new organic understanding of historic civilizations.

Though Niebuhr's book was a literary monster it was the first great work of modern historiography. Goethe characterized it well, and with it one of the fundamental educational values of the historical method, when he wrote to his friend Zelter: "Such a man's profound mind and active manner is really the thing that gives us strength. All these agrarian laws do not concern me at all. But the way he explains them and how he makes their complicated conditions clear to me is what enriches me and what places me under the obligation to act as conscientiously as he does in any business that I undertake."

Niebuhr showed what the new philological method could achieve in ancient history. He was the father both of modern *Altertumswissenschaft* and of critical modern historiography. Ranke and most other German historians of the first half of the nineteenth century were trained in classics, and the methods of criticism and interpretation which the scholars of the classics had developed formed the foundation of research in modern and medieval history. But one can equally well call Niebuhr's new "philological" method the critical historical method since it prepared the ground for a strictly historical treatment of the world of antiquity.

The German neohumanism of Winckelmann, F. A. Wolf, or Schiller had no longer approached the classics in the expectation of gaining ready-made and directly applicable precepts of life. The study of the classics was to them the means of experiencing the totality of natural human capacities and making them a power again in the building of a new civilization. As Schiller expressed it, the individual was to become a human being (*"das Individuum zum Menschen heraufzubilden"*), or to state this idea more freely, the individual was to realize his highest potentialities by the revival of his natural human capacities.

This *humanitas* was a classicist's ideal. But instead of a mere examination of the texts and monuments of the classical age, it called for an understanding of all the manifestations of Greek and Roman life as expressions of the spirit of classical civilizations. F. A. Wolf had demanded an encyclopedic study of antiquity, chiefly to provide the background for the interpretation of the works of classical literature. But once the inductive method, as used by Niebuhr, grew capable of analyzing and reconstructing the realities of classical life, it was soon discovered that the ideal Greek, in Boeckh's words, "lived on bread and wine" and not on "poetry and philosophy" and that "the Greeks were much unhappier than most people believe."

August Boeckh was the scholar who approached classic Greece as Niebuhr had studied Rome. His book on the *Public Economy of Athens* (1817) was dedicated to Niebuhr. For more than fifty years Boeckh was the most influential teacher and scholar of the classics in Germany. He drew clearly the conclusions from the new intellectual situation. Humanism was not the monopoly of the students of the classics. As he put it: "It is one of the presumptions of philologists, mostly unjustified by experience, that their study alone produces *humanitas*. This all studies must do if they are carried on truthfully, and in particular philosophy must do so. . . ."[5] Classical studies, or as Boeckh would say, "classical philology,"[6] are therefore only *one* way to reach an understanding of the potentialities of man. "The universal history of humanity presents the total unfolding of the powers with which the human spirit is endowed."[7]

Thus the absolute claims made for the study of the classics by the humanists were laid aside. The study of the classics became the "science of antiquity," the study of *one* of the historic civilizations, though of the most exemplary civilization and of the one that, together with Christianity, had produced the Western world. The ἀρχή or principle of our civilization, so often enshrouded in the later stages of history, could be grasped best in the study of antiquity. The methods of the classical studies, however, are identical with those of history. Boeckh said that "history was differentiated from philology only superficially, insofar as historians confine themselves mainly to the political life and treat the rest of the cultural life only in connection with the life of the state."[8]

Obviously Boeckh was not trying to set up a very sharp distinction between "philology" and history. He only points out a difference of emphasis in the academic discipline of his age. Actually today the conflict of which Boeckh was speaking would be defined as one between political and cultural history, and most historians would probably agree that political history is only a part of general cultural history, as Boeckh himself stated quite correctly. It should be mentioned that the program of Greek studies which Boeckh envisaged found its fulfillment in the work of a historian, in Jacob Burckhardt's *History of Greek Culture.* It was a historian again, J. G. Droysen, who first recognized the significance of the period of Greek history ushered in by Alexander's conquests, and described the period, hitherto looked upon as one of degeneration, as the productive "age of Hellenism." Again it was a historian, Theodor Mommsen, who dominated the field of classical scholarship after Boeckh's death, and in the life and work of von Wilamowitz-Moellendorf, Mommsen was undoubtedly the great formative influence.

These remarks are not intended to minimize the contributions made by those nineteenth-century scholars of the classics who concentrated on language, literature, or art exclusively. It should only be stressed that classical studies became historical studies after Niebuhr and Boeckh. Their present uncertainties and doubts with regard to their objectives are fundamentally those of the historical studies in general to which we shall have to turn our attention next.

IV

In considering the classical studies of the last century, a distinction should be drawn between creative scholarship and education in the classics. With regard to scholarship it can be said that the new historical approach, as developed in Germany in the early nineteenth century, proved irresistible and soon permeated the classical studies of all countries. But in general education the tradition of eighteenth-century classicism was not easily submerged. All over Europe, including Russia, classical teaching could maintain for most of the nineteenth century a privileged position as the gateway to any higher education and higher career. And everywhere the study of the classics was identified with humanism.

If we look at England we find that the eighteenth-century notion that the study of the classics would form the gentleman was not substantially changed in the Victorian age. This normative approach to the classics prevailed in English education and has continued to prevail, at least in Oxford and Cambridge, till very recently. The idea of learning by emulation still has a firm place in English classical teaching, though it was often superseded by the theory of the formalistic value of the classics, which meant that they trained the mind so effectively that it became capable of mastering any problem, e.g., the government of India or currency stabilization. The shift of emphasis from Roman to Greek studies that took place in English classical education did not affect the con-

tinued cultivation of ethical and social ideals. English humanism remained conscious of the individual's obligations to the
community, which meant not only to the British state but also
to the common brotherhood of men. The English humanism
of the last century was a great force working toward *humanitas* in the sense of φιλανθρωπία or humaneness.

In France, and similarly in Italy, so far as I can judge,
classical teaching was equally dominated by the older tradition. Naturally, Rome always remained closer to the Latin
countries than Greece, and humanistic studies were expected
to strengthen the national cultural tradition. But though political interest was not lacking, French humanism concentrated
upon literary rather than ethical ideals. The *littérateur* and
orator was the ideal of French classical education.

Classical scholarship and education were carried on in Germany under different theories. Ulrich von Wilamowitz-Moellendorff, in the opening paragraph of his *History of Philology*,
could write of "the philology which is still given the epithet
'classical,' though it no longer claims the pre-eminence implied by this name."[9] But this language was not heard in the
German "humanistic gymnasia," which during the nineteenth
century taught most of Germany's intelligentsia from what
corresponded to the period of the fourth or fifth grade in an
American public school through to the end of the sopho-
more year in college. The German "gymnasium" made no
contribution to the education of independent and responsible
citizens, nor did it inculcate very successfully humaneness
upon modern Germans. The best that the German "gymnasium" gave its pupils was the aesthetic revival of classic antiquity. In this respect, the spirit of Winckelmann, Schiller,
and the German eighteenth-century neohumanism lingered
on. But hardly ever did this lead to an appreciation of the
totality of classical civilization. The teaching was one-sidedly
concentrated on literature. Moreover, the "gymnasium" was
not really considered an end in itself but a preparation for the
university. The curriculum, therefore, was heavily burdened

with the teaching of language, grammar, and other auxiliary techniques. Nietzsche castigated the German "gymnasium" that gave its students the stones of classical science instead of the bread of a Greek philosophy of life.[10]

Whatever the merits of Nietzsche's own interpretation of classical civilization may have been, he was undoubtedly right in his general criticism. The classical school education of his age was a bowdlerized interpretation of classical civilization that passed over much of what could have served as a challenge to the modern world and the smug self-esteem of the nineteenth-century bourgeoisie. The classicist school system of nineteenth-century Europe was out of tune with the pulsating forces of a new age, and the disintegration of the old European society was one of the major causes of this school-bred humanism. Because of the democratic structure of the American school system this hybrid humanism found only a weak echo in the United States. Classical learning did not spread very far in nineteenth-century America, but on the other hand, she is unhampered by the traditionalism that kept Europeans from drawing the full consequences of the deep insights into the life of ancient civilization which the critical scholarship of the last century made possible.

This brings us back to scholarship in the classics, which we said became historical scholarship in the days of Niebuhr, Boeckh, Otfried Müller, and others. The expansion of our knowledge of antiquity has been tremendous. Ancient language, literature, arts, religion, philosophy, science, law, politics, and economy were covered ever more intensively. Simultaneously with the extension of the fields of study, the technical methods were improved and new ones created. Linguistics, metrics, epigraphy, papyrology, and archaeology came into being or were further perfected. With this vast increase of knowledge and techniques the original ideal of a knowledge of the totality of ancient civilization moved out of the reach of the individual scholar. As far as the mere coverage of the whole field of classical studies is concerned, some specialization is not ruinous. Boeckh quite correctly said: "Just in infiniteness lies the essence of scholarship, while only where the material is very limited—and even there not quite completely—does full comprehension become possible. Where infiniteness stops, scholarship comes to an end. Comprehension, however, is limited in length and breadth where an unending series [of problems] appears. In the dimension of depth scholarship can be fully realized. We can get so immersed in the singular that we grasp in it, as in a microcosm the whole, the macrocosm. In each individual idea we reach the whole, but no one can encompass all the ideas."[11]

Probably specialization is more baneful than Boeckh was ready to admit, but he was right in denying that the mere mastery of a technique could be called scholarship and that not even the study of an individual problem deserved the name of scholarship if it was not actively directed toward comprehensive understanding of human civilization as a whole.

Historical scholarship in the course of the later nineteenth century did not adhere to this theory of history. As a matter of fact, it was not given to the study and debate of methodology at all. The students of history went ahead with the reconstruction of the past without much philosophical argument. Most of them vaguely expected that once a large enough amount of detailed factual knowledge had been amassed the meaning of history as a whole would become clear, since it was inherent in the facts themselves. The study of civilizations became the aggregation of innumerable, so to speak, "photographic" reproductions of individual facts and episodes. This was declared to be the analogy to the inductive method as used in natural science. It is doubtful whether or not such a theory showed a right understanding of the practice of natural science, but it is certain that it was a fallacious theory for the cultural sciences.

Unquestionably, he who composes music needs sound or for that matter even pure tones, and no effort can be too great to enlarge the range and modulation of physical musical expression. But nobody will call the builder of instruments or the piano tuner composers, much as we may admire Guarneri or the men who developed the *Hammerklavier*. To write history without correct facts would be as preposterous as to write music without identifiable tones. But the knowledge of fact and detail does not constitute historical knowledge. We can understand just as much of the past as we can revive and relive in our own mind by the vicarious use of our own inner experience. But through history we overcome the limitations of our own temporary, local, and individual station in life and participate in man's rise from an animal state to civilization.

The individual grows not only by himself and from within but by acquiring the skills and wisdom of the community and by testing his own strength against social forces. The experience of the historicity of his own position and of all cultural forms enlarges immensely the awareness of both, the objective forces of history and the critical capacity of the individual. The growth of individuality, therefore, is bound up with the growing consciousness of the historic structure of human civilization. In this respect classical civilization still retains a strategic position for the education of Western man. No full understanding of Western civilization is possible without an understanding of ancient civilization. Western civilization is largely characterized by its roots in Greco-Roman civilization and by its continuous attempts to absorb the ideal contents of ancient civilization. This distinguishes Western from Russian civilization. It is very common to explain the difference of Western and Eastern civilization very largely by the absence of a Renaissance period. But in spite of the Byzantine link the classic tradition of Russia was never strong and the lack of a renascence can be easily explained. Russia never produced a scholasticism either.

The critical appreciation of ancient civilization, which has molded Western civilization, remains an essential task in our understanding of ourselves. Since classical civilization preceded the formation of the modern national cultures, it can also perform the function of a unifying bond of modern Western civilization. Moreover, in a period like the present, when all the civilizations of the world are brought face to face, the study of a civilization like the Greek, which is so much closer to the origins of civilization as such than our own derivative civilization, would be important for the understanding of foreign cultures as well. It seems to me that at the present moment it would be most desirable for classical scholarship to pay particular attention to the older as well as to the neighboring civilizations which helped to form Greek civilization. Equally the influence of Hellenic on the nascent Christian civilization is still one of the major problems not yet adequately dealt with in the interpretation of the history of Western civilization. Together with the problems mentioned earlier, it is one of the best approaches to an understanding of the meeting of civilizations.

History aims at an understanding of the totality of classical civilization. But since our own capacity to understand past civilizations is grounded in our own aliveness to the objective forms of human civilization, the historical approach to classical studies will divide into a number of approaches which follow the objectivations of human civilization. They are language, literature, the arts, religion, philosophy, science, law, politics, and economics. It has often been argued that language holds the key to all of these fields and on this claim high walls have been erected between philology, i.e., the approach through language, and history. Language is, indeed, as in most historical studies, the most powerful tool with which to penetrate into the classical world, and in many cases an entirely adequate means of achieving this end. It is to the credit of the classical scholars that they have not banned the classical philosophers, historians, and scientists from classical literature, as the students of modern literatures so often have done in their fields. On the other hand, language is the expression of human feeling, volition, and thinking, and the study of the documents and monuments of the history of civilization requires an understanding not only of the forms but also of the contents of the human mind.

The reconstruction and interpretation of Greek or Roman law for example has been furthered as much by the students of law as by the students of the classical languages. Or, to give another illustration, the full interpretation of Greek philosophy requires an active and creative philosophical talent. For centuries Aristotle's philosophy was studied from secondary sources, and Kantian teachings seemed to make any fresh and genuine study even more superfluous. It was Hegel who started a new interest in Aristotle, and Immanuel Bekker's critical edition of Aristotle would not have come into being without the philosophical movement of his day, as at present the existentialist philosophy may open new ways for the understanding of Greek philosophy.

Once we accept the view that our ability to understand the meaning of the past is dependent on our awareness of the driving forces of civilization, we shall not be inclined to give the scholar a monopoly of the classical heritage. Scholars are the chief curators of this cultural heritage, but only if they keep in contact with the creative work of the civilization of their own age will they be able to make important contributions to the understanding of the past. The actual influence of classical civilization upon our own civilization is not so much in the hands of scholars as of religious leaders, philosophers, artists, statesmen, etc. Even with respect to them the scholar has a critical function. Mussolini's sad caricature of Roman greatness would have been a proper subject of such criticism.

But if present-day classical scholarship wants to strengthen its grasp of antiquity it ought to go beyond the professional confines of academic learning. It must also contemplate the views of men like Hugo von Hofmannsthal, A. E. Housman, Thornton Wilder, T. S. Eliot, Eugene O'Neill, J. Anouilh, and others, in whose works the vision of classic life still manifests itself as a living force in the creative process of our own civilization.

INTRODUCING
THUCYDIDES

As THE Parthenon frieze or the statues of Praxiteles have not
ceased in two thousand years to be an inspiration to all lovers
of beauty, so the work of Thucydides still serves us as a
great source of wisdom on the growth and decline of civilizations. No one who wishes to understand the political forces
in history can afford to neglect the *History of the Peloponnesian War*. Thucydides was the first critical historical thinker
and writer to raise the study of history to a level comparable
to that of philosophy and science and his *History* constitutes
one of the most significant landmarks in the rise of Western
civilization. It is not surprising that many generations of
learned men have endeavored to explore its origins and contents. But what proves the true greatness of Thucydides' intellectual achievement is the power with which he speaks
not only to scholars but to everyone with an interest in history and politics.

A work of art transcends the limitations of its creator,
though it is at the same time the genuine expression of the
artist's personal experiences and feelings. Art is a form of
personal confession and it is by the transfiguration of his
own personality that the artist creates a new world for us. In
contrast, the historian is measured by the capacity for sub-
merging his private existence in the real world which he

wants to revive and understand. His personal contribution lies in the creation of patterns and forms through which he organizes the chaos of past events into a clearly discernible sequence and meaningful order. His own emotions are the means to breathe life into the events and men of the past.

Personal self-effacement was first shown by Thucydides to be the true prerequisite for the writing of critical history. It is, however, also the reason for the relative dearth of biographical data about him. On the whole we have to rely on the few remarks which Thucydides inserted in his book about himself. We may assume that he was born shortly after 460 B.C. the son of one of the great families of Athens. Through his father he was related to Miltiades, the victor of Marathon, and to his son Cimon, the leading Athenian statesman in the period before Pericles. Thucydides' father Olorus was a descendant of a local king in Thrace whose daughter Miltiades had married. In all likelihood Thucydides inherited the Thracian goldmines which, as he said, gave him a certain influence among the native Thracians. When in 424 B.C. Thucydides was elected one of the ten generals, i.e., a member of the board that acted for a year as the executive of Athens, these connections recommended him for a command in Thrace.

The important route to the Straits passed through this region, and the Spartans under Brasidas attempted to cut the artery of the Athenian Empire by an expedition against Amphipolis and the strategic Strymon valley. With only a small naval squadron at his disposal Thucydides failed to relieve Amphipolis in time. It was a stinging blow to the people of Athens and their leader Cleon was quick to turn their ire against the general. Thucydides was exiled and spent the next twenty years away from Athens, living mostly in Thrace but apparently traveling widely. His work displays not only familiarity with most parts of Greece but with Sicily as well. The fall of Athens in 404 B.C. made possible his return to the city. He survived the catastrophe of Athens by only a few years. He died probably in 399 B.C. or shortly thereafter. Only about two thirds of his *History,* covering the period to 411 B.C., were written, and the last, eighth book was still incomplete when he died.

These are the biographical facts which can be clearly established. Fortunately Thucydides' own work, viewed against the background of the general history of Greece, affords us a further key to his mind and character.

Thucydides grew up in the age which followed the Persian wars. Fighting together the Hellenes had repulsed the Persian invasion and maintained the freedom of their own states and civilization. But the experiences of common defeat and victory did not lead to lasting unity among them. The rise of Athens during the wars and her decisive contributions to the survival of the Greeks created a rivalry between herself and Sparta, the old leader of the Hellenes.

Athens had suffered grievously by the Persian invasion. The Persians had devastated both the countryside of Attica and the city and forced the Athenians into the sea. They took to the ships, while their women and children were evacuated to the islands. But the Athenian navy returned and annihilated the Persian fleet at Salamis in 480 B.C. and compelled Xerxes to evacuate Greece. These events demonstrated the need for naval power to thwart new Persian attempts at the subjugation of Greece. On the other hand, vast opportunities opened for Athens. Maritime occupations, shipbuilding, manufacture, and trading became the major pursuits of Athenian life. Probably few people ever went back to the rural life of prewar days and as a consequence the dominant position of the old landowning families declined. Navalism and empire-building were the forces which worked toward the transformation of the old oligarchic constitution of Athens into a democratic society.

The struggle over political rights within Athens consequently expressed itself in her foreign policy as well. The new social groups had grown prosperous in naval expansion and refused to abdicate when the danger from Persia subsided. What had begun as a heroic defense of Greece they wished to turn into an Athenian offensive against Persia. And when the Greek communities in the Aegean Sea showed signs of ending their acceptance of Athenian war leadership Athens did not hesitate to assert her imperial position.

But equally the relations between Athens and the Greek states on the mainland changed. Once the Greeks had welcomed the growth of Athenian naval might and considered it a shield of their own security and liberties. Sparta, being the chief landpower, seemed to offer a guarantee that Athens would never be able to turn her strength against the Greek commonwealth. However, the fortification of Athens and of her port, the Piraeus, made Athens unassailable from the land and signalized Athenian determination to assume an independent position in the Hellenic Confederacy. Soon major parts of central Greece were brought under the domination of Athens and the fight for the hegemony over Greece began.

Cimon, who represented the old landed aristocracy, tried in vain to confine the expansionist policy of Athens to the war against Persia in order to maintain the Hellenic Confederacy and friendly relations between Athens and Sparta, but he was ostracized in 461 B.C., shortly after the last checks against full democracy had been removed. During the next decade Athens not only conducted campaigns against Persia in Egypt but also tried to gain predominance among the Hellenes on the mainland. The two-front war ended disastrously and the young Pericles who emerged in this period as the leader of the new Athenian democracy learned his subsequent moderation by early defeat. Athens had to give up her attempts to exclude Persia completely from the Mediterranean and was deprived of most of her conquests in Greece by Sparta's intervention. A thirty years' peace between Athens and Sparta was concluded in 445 B.C., and though it recognized Athens as the second power of Hellas it limited the exuberant expansion of the city.

The peace allowed Athens to recover and for the time being she concentrated on the Aegean Sea, which remained her unchallenged sphere of influence. Athens forced her former allies to accept the position of subordinates. While in Athens ever larger groups of the people became politically enfranchized, the imperial rule of Athens over her satellites grew harsher as time went on. It was to prove one of the chief weaknesses of the Athenian Empire that it did not rest on the common loyalty and interest of its members for, unlike Rome, Athens did not grant citizenship to her subjects. The concentration of power in Athens and her growing commercial position in an orbit that reached from Sicily to the Straits made the uneasy balance between Sparta and Athens increasingly tenuous. The thirty years' peace lasted only fifteen years and in 431 B.C. war broke out again.

Thucydides tells us that he decided at once to write the history of this war "believing it to be great and memorable above any previous war." In spite of this clear statement it has often been asserted that only the misfortune of his exile made Thucydides a historian. But such a parallel to Machiavelli, who became a political and historical thinker after fate had crushed his career as an active statesman, is entirely fictitious. Thucydides himself merely mentions that his exile allowed him to extend to both sides his search for authentic reports on the events of the war. We may also assume that he gained time for his study and, most important, a more detached and objective viewpoint. Still, though we must believe that his ideas underwent some change due to the fortunes of his own life and to the cataclysmic course of the war, the original impulse for the writing of his *History* and the basic approach to the interpretation of the political events of his time date back to the earlier years of his life. As a member of one of the old Athenian families he must have participated since his youth in the political debates which kept Athens seething. And growing up at a time when Greek thought began to understand the world in rational terms he must also have started early to formulate his own political opinions on a conscious rational plane.

Thucydides moved in the political camp of Pericles, which seems unusual for one of Cimon's relatives, though Pericles himself came from the old nobility and Thucydides' formative years fell into the period when Pericles had modified the radical foreign policy of his early years. In any event, as in the case of Pericles, not birth but a conscious personal decision must have brought Thucydides to feel that the full realization of democracy was a desirable and practical aim. His *History* considers the democratization of Athens not only a natural and inevitable historical process but the primary cause of the vitality and greatness of Greek life in his time. The keen initiative of free citizens who knew that in war and in peace they carried forward their own personal cause had, in his opinion, produced the energy which made Athens more powerful at the beginning of the war than all of Hellas together had been at the time of the Persian wars. But Thucydides' admiration for the creative strength of democracy was tempered by the recognition of the tragic threat to Hellenic unity created by the growth of Athens. He also realized that democracy called for leadership capable of maintaining a steady and wise policy against irresponsible popular pressures.

The great political issues which dominated the Greek scene for the fifty years prior to the Peloponnesian War had doubtlessly been pondered by Thucydides before 431 B.C. when the outbreak of the war moved him to write history. In this respect, as in many others, he stood in sharp contrast to his predecessor Herodotus. The Ionian writer had been fascinated by the colorful variety of ethnographic phenomena which the wide world offered. Geographic exploration was as essential a part of his narrative as political history, and his chief desire to entertain and to spread useful general information. Compared to Herodotus the scope of Thucydides' interests seems much reduced. One looks in vain for a word on the classic civilization of Athens in the Periclean age, and Thucydides records no circumstances or events in the life of non-Athenian peoples which were unrelated to the drama of political power. The *History of the Peloponnesian War* was written by a statesman and political thinker for the political education of future generations.

Yet though the flowering of Athenian civilization did not form a major theme in the *History of the Peloponnesian War* the book itself was a shining manifestation of the spiritual revolution which took place in Athens during the fifth century. In fact, Thucydides was one of the greatest representatives of that singular generation of artists, scientists, and thinkers who made Greece the teacher of Rome and of the West in spite of her own political eclipse. His *History* is one of the mighty expressions of the new approach to the universe which the Greeks of this age discovered.

These Greeks put their faith in the power of human reason to understand nature and man by critical observation and analysis and believed that through such knowledge man's control over his environment could be enhanced. The old gods and faith were dethroned as the rulers of the world. Miracles were discarded in favor of rational interpretation built upon realistic investigation and logical argument. In general education this movement away from mythological toward rational thought was led by the sophists. It is also reflected in the development of the Greek drama from the religious art of Aeschylus through Sophocles to the psychological plays of Euripides. The same trend of thought is demonstrated in the new scientific medicine of the "Hippocratic" school which superseded magic healing. The historical thinking of Thucydides is the realization of similar ideas in politics. As a matter of fact, the analogies between Thucydides on one side and the sophists or Euripides or the scientists on the other are so close that Thucydides has been called at various times a mere emulator of one or the other of these schools. But such a judgment fails to describe his original contribution to Greek and Western thought.

Unquestionably Thucydides' intellectual growth was profoundly influenced by the general philosophical and artistic movement of the Periclean age. He thought many of the thoughts of the sophists and even modeled his style on theirs. It is also not difficult to find in his literary presentation the reflection of the Greek drama, while the exacting demands which the scientists had raised for the causal diagnosis of natural events were met in his circumspect analysis of political developments. But nowhere did Thucydides apply principles from other fields to the study of history in a mere mechanical fashion. Not only the definition of the field of historical study was all his own but he was original in the selection of the appropriate methods for its treatment. Deeply steeped in the wealth of creative ideas of his age he displayed a unique political discernment and historical clairvoyance which stemmed from the personal experiences of the Athenian citizen and soldier.

In the famous twenty-first and twenty-second chapters of the first book Thucydides expressed what in his opinion distinguished his work from those of his predecessors. He contrasted his own *History* with the historical writings of two groups of earlier authors, the poets and the chroniclers. The first, represented among others by Homer, he accused of "exaggerated fancies," the latter of seeking "to please the ear rather than to speak the truth." Rightly he included undoubtedly his greatest forerunner, Herodotus, among those prose writers who chiefly wrote to entertain. Their search for historical truth was limited by their literary aims which made the preservation of legendary tradition rather attractive.

Thucydides demanded the complete removal of legends from history. It was his belief that history could not be written without contemporary sources which he found chiefly in direct eye- and ear-witness accounts. Since they often disagreed "as they remembered or were interested in the actions of one side or the other" they had to be critically weighed and sifted. However, since sources of this type did not exist for older Greek history and in the poetic or rhetoric tradition events of the past soon passed into the realm of the mythical, Thucydides considered it impossible to reconstruct the full history of the past. Only some "general conclusions" could be drawn from the available evidence. In the first twenty chapters of his work he illustrated the character of such general conclusions.

Leopold Ranke, the greatest among nineteenth-century historians, liked to muse about the difference between ancient and modern historiography and he saw one of the major distinctions in Thucydides' ability to write the history of his own times with objective detachment while modern historical writers had proved incapable of an objective treatment of contemporary history. Ranke, incidentally, all through his life gave his attention not only to his universal studies of the past but also to the history of his own time to which he made in fact some valuable contributions. Most nineteenth-century historians declared the present and the recent past as outside of the domain of critical study and would have subscribed to Mommsen's statement: "The act in the drama of history that we attend and ourselves help more or less to stage as actors or supernumeraries—that act we live through but do not understand. Only when the mighty life has grown silent history begins."

The greatness of Thucydides lies in his unmatched achievement of a critical understanding of the events of his own age though he lived through them with a passionate heart. The contrast between intense human emotions as recaptured in the realistic narrative and the almost pitiless appraisal of the objective significance of the events constitutes the fascination of Thucydides' *History*. At first sight it may seem strange that it was the burning desire of the statesman to assess the forces with which he was struggling that carried him beyond the actual conflict. But the world of politics is not a world of sheer subjectivity as most people believe. In reality, there is no greater nor severer school where men can learn the narrow bounds of mere subjective thought and action. The statesman or general who gives his personal sentiments free rein is likely to misjudge the actual strength of his position and to underrate the power of his enemies and will be quickly defeated. One of the fundamental criteria of political leadership is the capacity for meeting situations not only with subjective conviction but with calmly calculating reason.

In an epoch when commanders refused to accept battle if the auguries failed and historical writers continued to believe in the direct intervention of the gods Thucydides boldly conceived of history as the domain of men. And imbued with the faith of the philosophical age he maintained that man was not only born to act and suffer according to his blind passions but also to acquire knowledge with which he could hope to improve the power over his environment. Through the presentation of a crucial stage of history Thucydides attempted for the first time to prove that historical events were not determined by magic influences but by human nature itself and that the actions and reactions of human beings could be studied by critical observation from which future generations would profit. Thus he proclaimed: "And very likely the strictly historical character of my narrative may be disappointing to the ear. But if he who desires to have before his eyes a true picture of the events which have happened, and of the like events which may be expected to happen hereafter in the order of human things, shall pronounce what I have written useful then I shall be satisfied. My history is an everlasting possession, not a prize composition which is heard and forgotten."

This was not a proud claim for literary immortality but the expression of his belief in the historian's ability to establish truth which would be valid for all time to come and would, therefore, be found "useful" by future generations.

The historical pragmatism of Thucydides rested on the assumption that history might vary somewhat but that the problems of each age would be similar in character. The problem of the uniqueness of historical events which has been so much emphasized, and perhaps overemphasized, in modern philosophy of history, was of little concern to him. Nor did he make any attempt to understand the history of the human race as a unified process in which each epoch becomes a stepping stone to the succeeding age. One might perhaps expect a historical thinker convinced of the "everlasting" function of reason to develop a theory of human history as progress toward societies possessed of expanding knowledge. But such speculation was alien to Thucydides. His purpose was much more practical.

On the one hand he intended to describe accurately important phenomena which had occurred so that they could be recognized easily if they appeared again. He justifies for example in such terms his detailed narration of the plague which proved one of the contributing causes of Athens' downfall. On the other hand he drew certain conclusions about the impact of events on men, such as his statement that "in peace and prosperity both states and individuals are actuated by higher motives, because they do not fall under the dominion of imperious necessities; but war which takes away the comfortable provision of daily life is a hard master and tends to assimilate men's characters to their conditions."

The Greek doctors of the Hippocratic school had cultivated the descriptive study of illnesses and their symptoms, thus attempting to lay the basis for the correct identification of their causes and the selection of the right therapeutic treatment. In analogous fashion the accurate description of political developments and problems was to prepare the statesman for his task of political leadership. Thucydides left no doubt about the qualities which in his opinion made the great statesman. Speaking of the victor of Salamis and founder of the Athenian Empire, Themistocles, he praised above all the former's ability to reach quick policy decisions even in new and unexpected circumstances, his foresight of future developments, and his power of clarifying political issues to others. But Thucydides emphasized that Themistocles was an extraordinary figure insofar as he was endowed with these gifts by nature and had not acquired them by study and reflection.

In the admiring treatment of Pericles it becomes clear that Thucydides placed his foremost trust in those leaders whose statecraft was not merely rooted in their intuitive faculties but also founded on knowledge. Those who have studied history will not be perplexed by events which have occurred in similar form in earlier times. They will be able to meet them boldly, while those who have no knowledge of the past are likely to be frightened into accepting such occurrences as the freaks of unconquerable fate. For, as Thucydides remarked, both the mass of the people and their leaders are prone to ascribe so much to fate since they lack knowledge and cannot think resolutely. Thucydides did not assert that all events were comprehensible or traceable to rational causes, but he regarded it as possible to extend the province of human reason in politics and thereby enhance the statesman's wisdom in guiding the destinies of state.

Thucydides was far from suggesting that the lessons of history could be compressed into a few principles. Only through a review of the totality of the events and of their full complexity could an insight be gained into the deeper causes of the historical process. Then distinctions could be drawn between the purely momentary and the lasting effects, between the individual and the generic forces, between the necessity imposed on mortal human beings from the outside and that tragic necessity which springs from man's nature itself, from his reckless appetites, his far-flung ideals as much as from his nebulous vision and his superstitions. Thucydides' concern about the accuracy of research has to be seen in conjunction with these wider aims. Insistence upon accuracy by itself would only have led to the compilation of a better chronicle than those formerly composed. Thucydides, however, wanted to do more than to collect facts. He wished to present a decisive chapter of history to illuminate the operation of deep underlying causes as clearly as the human mind could perceive them.

This general objective was also the rule for selecting the essential facts from the mass of irrelevant information. Thucydides obviously refused to narrate for the sake of narration and he scorned mere literary ornament and redundancy. Indeed, he has been criticized with a certain right for having chosen too small a canvas for the great panorama he presented. His chapters and sentences are packed with meaningful references and it is by no means easy to follow him at all times, the more so since the Greek language of his day had not yet reached that subtlety and richness of form characteristic of the Greek prose of later periods. And still, the terseness and compactness of the Thucydidean style is the true expression of a man devoted to great matters and high ideas. It has been correctly said that everybody who spends time to decipher one of Thucydides' more recondite words or sentences will be rewarded not merely by grammatical and literary knowledge but will always grasp a new idea as well. There is in the conciseness of his presentation and in his personal reticence an uncanny appeal that heightens the tension of the historical drama which he unfolds and compels his readers to higher personal sympathy and thought. Macaulay, himself a master of an appealing literary prose, confessed repeatedly that no historian could ever hope to match the power of Thucydides' presentation.

After a review of the older history of Greece, Thucydides begins his narrative with a description of the circumstances which led to the outbreak of the war between Sparta and Athens in 431 B.C. Corinth, strategically placed on the isthmus that links the Peloponnesus with the Greek mainland and separates the Aegean Sea from the western Mediterranean, had lost her role as the leading naval power of

Greece by the rise of Athens and Athenian control of the Aegean. Corinth tried to recover her position by expansion in the west and as a first step in this direction endeavored to subjugate her former colony Corcyra, a natural maritime bastion commanding the trade route to Italy. The Corcyreans in 433 B.C. had countered the policy of Corinth by requesting to join the Athenian federation. Athens acted correctly and granted Corcyra only a defensive alliance and avoided having her navy directly intervene in the struggle between Corinth and Corcyra. But a conquest of Corcyra by Corinth was now impossible. Corinth, her western policy blocked, turned to direct intervention in the affairs of the Athenian Empire. When Potidaea, another colony of Corinth, which however had become a member of the Athenian federation, attempted to secede from the federation Corinth actively supported the secessionists.

This was a clear breach of the peace of 445 B.C. and hostilities opened in the northern Aegean which led to years of fighting. But only the intervention of Sparta turned the conflict between Corinth and Athens into a general Hellenic war. Thucydides draws a clear line between the occasion which led to the Peloponnesian War and its real causes. He is careful to point out that the Athenian policy of this time kept on the whole within the bounds of the existing treaties and that it was Sparta that refused to accept an arbitration of the conflict as provided for in the treaty of 445 B.C. But Thucydides characterizes the war as inevitable. In his opinion it was caused by Sparta's understandable fear of the growth of Athens' might. Sparta was the power of the status quo in Greece. She had continued in the old forms of agricultural economy and could not hope to compete in commercial rivalry. Nor could she ever expect to acquire greater strength than she had gained by the rigid organization of her national life. Her oligarchic constitution had proved stable even in days when all other Greek states had been torn asunder by civil strife. Yet ruling over a large population of subjected helots Sparta was afraid of their defection in adversity and this was bound to discourage a venturesome policy.

It would be wrong to say that Sparta was resting on her laurels, since there was no slackening of communal effort and discipline. But she did not create novel ideas or policies. Her interests demanded the preservation of the old order of Greece which was the best protection of her own hegemony and of her traditional social structure. The startling growth of Athens as a commercial and maritime power threatened to upset the precarious balance on which Sparta's leadership depended. Though she was not directly challenged by Athens she found it impossible to resist the requests for help from her allies.

As Thucydides described the motives of Spartan action as conditioned by her economic and political institutions he likewise explained Athens' policy and character as the outcome of her naval exploits and her new political and social life. Athens was the great innovator which in taking to the sea had acquired energies never before realized in Hellenic history. But she also had left the accustomed shores of older Greek thought. And in this connection our earlier statement that Thucydides paid no attention to the civilization of Athens should be modified. It is true that names like Phidias, Euripides, Anaxagoras, or Protagoras do not appear in the *History* and that no great work of art of the period is praised. The Acropolis is mentioned as the Athenian treasury and the glorious Propylaea as a building whose construction had eaten deeply into the reserve funds of the city-state. But Thucydides saw in the flowering of culture one of the great achievements of Athenian democracy and in the Funeral Speech of Pericles his own pride in the creativeness of Athens found a sounding expression.

Thucydides, in contrast to many a modern admirer of Greek art and literature, was conscious of the degree to which the new Athenian culture depended on the political and social life of the city. He knew that the same wealth that poured in the coffers of Athens enabled her both to bring forth a world of beauty and to fight her wars against most of Hellas. He also knew that this affluence had freed the Athenians from the necessity of maintaining their society like that of Sparta on a permanent warfooting. They could abolish the daily restraints which Sparta imposed on her citizens and become tolerant of the individual's thought and action, as long as they did not violate the communal laws and traditions. The authoritarian philosophy of Sparta believed that men could be made efficient and useful only by continuous supervision and training. Athens held to a liberal faith in the free pursuit of beauty, independent thought, and even the mere amenities of life, trusting that the greater vitality thus developed would make her citizens in times of need "as brave as those who never allow themselves to rest."

Civilization had a central place in Thucydides' thinking, though within the framework of his *History* he was content with showing only its ultimate basis which he found in political power, and with demonstrating its action as a ferment of political life. In principle Thucydides' methods still seem sound after more than two thousand years. He analyzed the economic resources and the social structure of a state and related them to the political institutions which determined the national character and the ideas of its citizens, and finally studied the part played by these ideas in the practical use of the power of the state.

It is at this point where another and no less important train of thought begins. Thucydides was convinced that Athens on account both of her material and spiritual wealth could have won the war and replaced Sparta as the leader of Greece if she had used her power wisely. But although democracy by its stimulation of initiative sets free vaster energies and higher vision than oligarchy, it is at the same time exposed to much greater dangers. Due to the unlimited discussion of all issues there is in democracy a greater reasoning power, but there is also an increased intensity of public and private passions which may bring reason to nought.

The fundamental problem of a commonwealth is how to control the divergent forces by prudence, and Thucydides finds the answer largely in leadership. Largely, but by no means exclusively, for in the eyes of Thucydides the decline of Athens was not only due to the deterioration of her leadership but equally to the diminishing capacity of the people to recognize the best interests of the community and to live up to their responsibilities. Thucydides did not share the view of the champions of oligarchy in Sparta and Athens who decried democracy as the rule of the lower classes. Democracy meant to him the participation of all the people in the discussion and formulation of policies, and he saw in this the ideal form of government. But it called for leaders who were devoted to the public weal and able to recognize the common interest of the state. At the beginning of the Peloponnesian War, Athens was fortunate in having a united people and a statesman of ideal stature. Pericles combined absolute personal integrity and patriotism with the qualities which, as we already saw, Thucydides considered the prerequisites of political leadership, namely the power of objective analysis, foresight, and political argument in public debate.

He represented the national spirit of Athens in its highest form and his personal probity together with his political acumen placed him in a position where he could lead the people rather than being led by them, where he could advocate unpopular measures and make the people support long-range policies based on a full understanding of national needs. In a rare hyperbolic statement that betrays his personal admiration of Pericles, Thucydides said that Athens, though nominally a democracy, was actually led by its first citizen. The statement has often been interpreted as an indication of his relative faith in democracy, but for no good reason. Thucydides emphasized that Pericles ruled the Athenians "without limiting their freedom" and without changing their democratic institutions. Obviously he saw in the rule of Pericles the supreme fulfillment of democracy which was the willingness of free and thinking men to follow a great leader in a wise course of action whatever the price might be. The history of Athens' fall was the history of the decay of her public spirit and her leadership.

Thucydides regarded Pericles' appraisal of the war situation as correct and fully borne out by subsequent events. Pericles judged that the power of Athens was adequate to resist the onslaught of Sparta and her Peloponnesian allies. However, in view of the Spartan superiority on land the Athenians could not afford to meet the Spartans in open land battle. They had to evacuate the countryside of Attica and withdraw its population behind the walls of the impregnable city. Neither Athens nor her island empire could be successfully attacked by the Spartans since Athens ruled supreme on the sea. And the great mobility which naval power afforded permitted Athens to keep her enemies on their toes and to inflict losses on them by raids into the Peloponnesus. On the whole Pericles proposed a defensive strategy of attrition based on the strength of Athens' financial and economic resources which her foes could not hope to match for any length of time. But Athens could fail if she strained her might unnecessarily, particularly if she started on imperial conquests while the war lasted.

The strategy which ruled more or less the first seven years of the war required for its success moderation and discipline at home. But soon there were indications of a deterioration of the unity and prudence of the Athenians. The evacuation of Attica and its devastation by Spartan invasion and the grave inconveniences created in the overcrowded city caused considerable grumbling, but the outbreak of the plague during the second year of the war produced fear and licentiousness. The craving for personal advantage and private pleasures ruined the sense of public service, and negotiators were sent to Sparta. The social and moral consequences of the plague, which probably took away up to a third of the population of Athens, were understandable, but the event showed that the rational soundness of the war plan by itself would not decide the outcome of the war.

Yet the first crisis passed. Though Pericles died a few months later, himself a victim of the plague, the war was fought for four more years according to his plan, showing year for year the same general picture of Spartan invasions of Attica and seaborne operations of the Athenians against the Peloponnesus. Finally in 425 B.C. the Athenians succeeded in cutting off a sizable force of Spartan fighters on the island of Sphacteria, and Sparta, dreading the loss of a valuable group of her hoplites and tired of a war in which she did not know how to force a decision, offered peace and an alliance to Athens. The offer was in fact a full consummation of the original war aims of Athens, but Cleon, now her leading statesman, aroused the Athenians to decline the offer by demanding the Athenian possessions on the Greek mainland which Athens had ceded in the treaty of 445 B.C. Sparta was willing to grant parity but not hegemony to Athens. Fighting was resumed and the Spartans, under the able and bold Brasidas, succeeded for the first time in threatening Athenian control of the northern Aegean by the capture of Amphipolis. Cleon himself had to try to redeem this position. He failed and was killed in the attempt, but Brasidas also gave his life in the battle. With the leaders of the war parties gone a peace was negotiated between the two states. The so-called Peace of Nicias of 421 B.C. was a return to the status of 431 B.C. Pericles seemed justified.

But the Athens of 421 B.C. was no longer the Athens of Pericles. All the elements which had made Athens the potentially greatest state of Greece showed signs of decay. The unity of common debate and action, the prevalence of reason in the councils of state, and a leadership whose exclusive aims were the preservation of the democratic institutions and the security of the city had been gravely endangered in the years after Pericles' death. The impact of the plague was after all not just a passing episode but a serious prelude to the social devastation that the strains of a long war were bound to create among the people. Wild passions were engendered which soon confused the great issues of the war, since few people liked to listen to reason any longer. In these conditions the leadership of the state fell into the hands of persons like Cleon who played upon the emotions of the people to build up a selfish personal rule. Under Cleon, Athenian democracy was no longer the government by all the people but the domination of the lower classes through wily demagogues. By the appeal to the prejudices and superstitions of the masses, by questioning education, and by slandering the motives of opponents well-reasoned arguments were squashed. And with reason and moderation respect for law and humaneness was ruined. The ideals of the Periclean age were ridiculed and so was his war program. When the Spartans offered what Pericles had defined as peace aims Cleon was able to thwart the peace. The mood of the Athenians had turned imperialist.

There was no change of heart after Cleon's death, the more so since the Peace of Nicias was never executed. Sparta's smaller allies balked at the restoration of certain places to Athens, whereupon Athens refused to carry out all provisions of the treaty. Intermittent fighting continued all through the years of "peace" from 421 to 416 B.C. when the full fury of war started again. The Athenians entered this stage in an attitude of reckless power politics. The brutal conquest and destruction of Melos, an Aegean island which had maintained neutrality in the war, showed the cynicism to which Athenian policy had fallen. In this spirit they decided upon the boldest plan to win the war by an extension of their empire into the western Mediterranean. The conquest of Syracuse and Sicily was to add the wealth of that island to their resources, and once this was accomplished Athens could hope to crush Sparta. The plan was not necessarily a mere gamble, provided it had the full support of the people and was ably carried out. Popular enthusiasm was not lacking; in fact never before had Athens fitted out such an imposing naval and military force.

Athens also had the man capable of directing such a daring campaign. Alcibiades, the father of the plan, had the mental qualities of a great statesman and commander, political perspicacity, and the gift of exposition to a high degree. Still he was lacking in unselfishness and patriotism which had made Pericles so strong in the estimate of the people. The pomp and license of his personal life had aroused many suspicions against the erstwhile pupil of Socrates. How different was the other outstanding political figure of this time, Nicias! He was patriotic and entirely devoted to his duties, but his world was rather pre-Periclean. A conservative, leaning toward oligarchy, he resented the imperialist expansion of Athens and in particular regarded the Sicilian expedition as a frightful risk. In action he was too meticulous and without great vision.

It was clear that once Alcibiades' strategy had been approved, no other man could have brought it to fruition. Together with Nicias he was elected chief of the expedition, but, accused as an accomplice in the sacrilegious outrages which had happened on the eve of the departure of the fleet, he was recalled to stand trial. Instead he went to Sparta. Athens had driven her foremost statesman into the camp of the enemy and at the same time crippled her supreme effort to gain victory in Sicily. Nicias was incapable of using the Athenian forces to the best advantage. He finally recommended withdrawal, simultaneously offering his resignation. Against his advice the Athenians decided to hold on, but they did not replace Nicias. The reinforcements they sent did not change the strategic situation. Nicias was fearful to take it upon himself to order the retreat while there was time. He dreaded the anger of the demos and was influenced by auguries.

Thus total catastrophe overtook the Athenian forces. At

one stroke Athens lost not only one of her best armies but, even worse, her entire navy with all the skill of its trained officers and sailors. The very foundations of the Athenian empire were shaken and, with Syracuse joined to the Peloponnesians, Athens appeared doomed to ignominious defeat. But even now Athens' power and fighting spirit were not broken. In spite of her disastrous losses and continuing internal strife Athens stayed in the war for seven more years, still at times gaining brilliant victories. Sparta, though reinforced by Syracuse, had to turn to Persia for the development of a navy adequate to subdue Athens' maritime strength. The price paid by Sparta to win Persia's financial help, the sacrifice of Greek cities in Asia Minor to Persian rule, shattered her moral claim to be the protector of Greek freedom.

Thucydides had only sketched out the events of the first two years after the Sicilian debacle when he died. Posterity suffered a grievous loss by being deprived of his treatment of the final acts of the war. No doubt Thucydides would have found in the scenes of flickering hope, mounting violence and despair, which characterize the last stage of the war, subjects he would have been able to transform into masterful visions of the nature of political life. But though these chapters of his work would in all probability have equaled the earlier ones, it is impossible to assume that they could have surpassed them. No historical events, for example, could have been brought to fuller life than the Sicilian expedition. Every reader will follow with breathless suspense the unfolding drama. He is prepared to understand the motives and aims of the peoples and individuals, he witnesses the actual toil and agony of battle and sees the circumstances and incidents of war as well as their reaction on men in their courage, determination, and blindness. These are some of the elements out of which the drama is woven, its tragic sense emerging not from the intervention of outside forces but rather from the inner conflict of human nature.

Although Thucydides aimed at, and achieved, the realistic

revival of actual occurrences they were to him not only extraordinary experiences of the human race but also prototypes of future events. Modern historical interpretation, in contrast to Thucydides, would stress the singular character of any historical age and would also be congnizant of a greater potentiality of man to change. But not even our contemporary world would consider a historical work generally important unless it helped to illuminate something beyond the individual subject-matter it presents. We do not believe that the study of an individual epoch could give us a full insight into human nature but we are inclined to view each period as a link in the comprehensive chain of human events.

Thus we may disagree with Thucydides' assumption that a single age could encompass the range of human potentialities, but we still believe that the study of history should lead to a better and more objective understanding of the totality of human nature. And Thucydides was the first historian who fully realized that such historical understanding can be gained only by entering into the minds of the actors. The explanation of their conscious and half-conscious thoughts is the key to a sympathetic appraisal of their intentions and motives. The vividness of Thucydides' work rests to a large extent in his ability to record the changing ideas of an age of political and intellectual crisis.

Thucydides distinguished two major categories of historical phenomena: things done and things said, or actions and speeches. The latter served Thucydides to present the thought and ideas of the states and individuals. But he admitted that neither he himself nor other witnesses had been able to remember the exact wording of the speeches and he continued by saying: "I have therefore put into the mouth of each speaker the sentiments proper to the occasion, expressed as I thought he would be likely to express them, while at the same time I endeavored, as nearly as I could, to give the general purport of what was actually said." If with regard to events Thucydides proclaimed the utmost critical accuracy as the ideal historical method, he practiced a different method in the rendition of speeches. He did not consider it admissible, like Herodotus, to invent speeches where all evidence for their delivery was lacking. He also demanded that the intention and personality of the speaker should be correctly reflected. But Thucydides acknowledged that actual speeches could not be fully reconstructed from the reports of listeners and that, therefore, he had the speakers express what in his own opinion the situation demanded.

Practically all ancient historians adopted the Thucydidean manner of inserting speeches in their narratives and so did most of the modern historians, till Voltaire objected to such "oratorical lies" and "fictions." Modern historians feel that without authentic texts of the speeches at his disposal Thucydides ought to have given only their general character. But the speeches of Thucydides were not, as those by many of his successors, free exercises in rhetoric but aimed at the discovery of a higher truth. Thucydides was convinced that each historical situation was dominated by an inner logic of its own. Sentiments "proper to the occasion" consequently were not fictitious embellishments of the events invented by the historian but the expressions of the underlying motives of action as they arose with logical necessity. Therefore he used the speeches not only to characterize the driving forces of action but also to demonstrate his own interpretation of history. In a few remarkable places of the book he stated his historical judgment directly, as modern historians would prefer to do, but in general his appraisal of the course of events was merged into the speeches.

Thucydides was the true son of the Greece of his age. To the Hellenes political life was actually divided into actions and speeches. It reached the same intensity in their democratic and oligarchic councils as on the battlefield, and the culture of speech had already reached a considerable level. If Thucydides had treated the councils of state and the art of speechmaking in a summary fashion he would have appeared unrealistic in Greek eyes. Moreover with regard to the presentation of his own ideas it should be noted that Thucydides did not, like our modern historians, fall heir to literary forms in which an author's reasoning could be couched in a versatile prose. But the great Greek drama of his time had created the capacity for making visible a general and ideal type in the individual event, the very problem that the historian had to meet.

Small wonder then that Thucydides was deeply attracted by the literary opportunity offered by speeches. The ideas which in Thucydides' view could be derived from the events were used to heighten the dramatic character of his *History*. The great critical moments of the war, such as its eve, or the time before the decision to embark upon the Sicilian expedition, were the chief occasions for speeches and in them the meaning of such historic hours was made transparent. Thucydides also artfully employed another potential advantage of the dramatic method. With the speeches of Pericles being the major exception he liked to introduce pairs of speeches to remind the reader of the perspective nature of truth and the dialectic process of history. Once we see him use instead the dialogue form: in the debate between the Athenians and Melians where Thucydides depicted the Athenians in their brazen state of imperialism and showed the eternal conflict between might and right in a scene that will never be matched in its painful poignancy.

Thucydides, however, avoided following the dramatists in using speeches to build up the human individual as such. Even the outstanding leaders like Pericles, Cleon, or Alcibiades were drawn only with a view to their political attitude and ability, and even they remain representatives of their political groups or states. The speeches, therefore, were not mere portraits but characterizations of the collective entities which Thucydides saw struggling in history. Foremost among them was, of course, the contrast between the national attitudes of Sparta and Athens upon which light was thrown from every angle. Thucydides used the device of introducing these two protagonists first through the description of the impression they made on the other states of Greece. In the case of Athens it was fear and jealousy which determined the language of the Corinthian speakers. Against this background the glorious three Periclean speeches stand out, particularly the Funeral Speech, the immortal praise of democracy to which no better historical parallel exists than the Gettysburg Address.

As Thucydides here compared and illustrated national characters he confronted in other speeches social and political factions. The debates between Cleon and Diodotus or between Nicias and Alcibiades are examples. But at the same time there are running through all speeches certain *leitmotivs* which represent the historical wisdom of Thucydides. By throwing the thoughts and motives of the actors into bold relief he speaks his own considered judgment. The speeches are, therefore, not only the crucial links of his narrative but also of his historical evaluation.

The literary methods of Thucydides are no longer a direct model for historical writers. But it should not be forgotten that the division of history into actions and speeches was more realistic in the fifth century B.C. than at any other period of Western civilization and that even modern historians, by quoting some high points of a historic speech, are to some extent giving an implicit interpretation.

Thucydides has remained through the centuries not only one of the precursors of modern historical research but the founder of some of its major principles. No other historian can claim to have achieved as much for the critical understanding of history as Thucydides did in his age. Through the centuries Tacitus, Machiavelli, Hobbes, Ranke, and Macaulay recognized him as the incomparable master of the historical study of politics, and no doubt his great thoughts will live as long as men strive to gain an objective view of history and believe that reason strengthens their hands against blind fate.

Our generation contemplating the material and moral wreckage left in the wake of the recent war will read Thucydides' study of the impact of war upon the life of civilized nations with a new admiration for his profound wisdom. Citizens of democratic states will find in his work one of the monumental descriptions of the power of democracy to set free the energies of its citizens and to gain strength through freedom. Thucydides, however, was not only aware of the glories which democracy could produce but also of its perils. He saw democracy continuously endangered by the conflict between emotions and reason, between factional interests and the common good, and analyzed how this conflict was aggravated by the acquisition of empire which could lead to an unbearable tension between the freedom at home and domineering control abroad. His work is, indeed, an "everlasting possession."

GREEK AND MODERN
CONCEPTS OF HISTORY*

ONLY IN THE Hellenic and Western civilization did historical thought acquire a truly fundamental role for the whole structure of culture. A desire to retain some memories of the past is common to all civilizations, but only a small number of them developed a form of historical interest that went beyond mythology, and even fewer reached the stage on which we find factual state chronicles or official annals and, on the other side, a novelistic treatment of unusual historical episodes. The Old Testament shows all these forms side by side in the mythological speculations of the Genesis, the chronicles of kings, and in such stories as those of Samson and David. The same types of historical writing can be found in Babylonian and Egyptian literature as well as in Greece.

The Greeks, however, rose to a new level of historical thought that left the mythological interpretation and also the annalistic and novelistic presentation of history far behind. Almost simultaneously with the birth of natural science, which superseded the ancient cosmology, the new critical history came into being. Thucydides defined the task of this new history in the famous twenty-second chapter of the first book of his *Peloponnesian War*. Its last two sentences read:

* This paper formed part of a symposium held before the Fullerton Club at Bryn Mawr College, May 10, 1947.

". . . and it may well be that the absence of the fabulous from my narrative will seem less pleasing to the ear; but whoever shall wish to have a clear view both of the events which have happened and of those which will some day, in all human probability, happen again in the same or a similar way—for these to adjudge my history useful will be enough for me. And, indeed, it has been composed, not as a prize essay to be heard for the moment, but a possession for all time."

Practically every word in these sentences is charged with a philosophical meaning. With conscious determination Thucydides excluded myth and poetry and also disapproved of a literary or rhetorical appeal to the aesthetic imagination. The historian was concerned with objective knowledge to be gained through the collection and critical analysis of authentic sources. If Thucydides called his work an "everlasting possession" he was not raising a claim to literary immortality but stating his conviction that historical research could yield truth valid for the future, and knowledge "useful" for the management of human affairs.

Thucydides became a historian out of political passion. A son of the old Athenian nobility, he was compelled to find an answer to the revolutionary developments which had taken place in Athens as a consequence of the Persian invasion of 480 B.C. The Persians had literally pushed the Athenians from the mainland to which they returned as naval conquerors. Probably few Athenians ever went back to the Attican countryside, thus depriving the ancient stronghold of the nobility of its former significance. Instead the Athenians developed an urban society in which commercial and maritime interests began to dominate. The decline of the oligarchy and the growth of democracy were the natural results.

The outlook of the new classes also changed the foreign policy of Athens. The rise of Athens as the naval power of the Aegean was welcomed by the other Greek states so long as Athenian policy aimed at the protection of Greek freedom against Persia. But soon the new classes started employing Athens' strength for their own acquisitive ends, irrespective of the Greek common weal. Cimon was the last Athenian statesman who tried to check the further democratization of the city and to conduct a foreign policy that would have avoided the open clash between Athenian and Greek interests. He failed and another member of the nobility, Pericles, assumed the leadership. Pericles introduced full democracy and, in his early period, was identified with a policy of imperialist expansion which almost ended in disaster for the city. But he took his lesson to heart and became the representative of a foreign policy of limited objectives, and he formulated the strategy of Athens with prudent moderation after the outbreak of the Peloponnesian War.

Thucydides grew up in the midst of these political controversies and embraced the Periclean program. He must have felt like Pericles that the new democratic forces could not be repressed and that they constituted the source of the vitality that had multiplied the power of Athens. But democracy needed leaders who would be able to curb its excesses and steer a wise course in foreign affairs.

Thucydides described two great leaders of Athens, Themistocles and Pericles. He called Themistocles great because he was capable of reaching policy decisions quickly, even in new and baffling circumstances, because he had a foresight of future developments, and because he was able to clarify political issues for others. But the historian added that in Themistocles these gifts had been the mere expression of his "natural force" and had not been supported by reflection and study. In the corresponding treatment of Pericles Thucydides depicts the ideal statesman as the one who acts not only by intuition but also through knowledge. Such a leader will not mistake recurring events as novel incidents. Many occurrences which are commonly considered manifestations of chance and, therefore, beyond human control can be traced to rational causes and countered by appropriate political action. Although

Thucydides was far from denying the role of fate altogether, he believed that the critical study of history offered a method for extending the human understanding of the political forces and thus for enhancing the wisdom of statesmen guiding the destinies of nations.

Thucydides shared the conviction of the Greek philosophers, scientists, and poets of his age that the power of reason could free men from a superstitious belief in blind fate or the play of supernatural forces. Historical life was a self-contained human process not interfered with by the gods. The parallel to the teachings of the so-called Hippocratic school of medicine is striking. By a careful study of the symptoms of illnesses the school attempted to reach a critical understanding of their causes, thus replacing magic therapeutics by a scientific medicine. It would be erroneous to assume that Thucydides mechanically applied the Hippocratean scheme to politics. Both the medicine of Hippocrates and the history of Thucydides are expressions of a deeper current of Greek intellectual life in that period.

It is, however, true that Thucydides became a historian because he held that the study of history was the approach to a critical understanding of politics. In his view history and political science were identical. This did not mean that history could produce simple laws and lessons. But a higher insight into politics could be gained only by reliving history in its concreteness. The reconstruction of the past events in their true historical sequence and realistic color was the first task of the historian and only through the compassionate contemplation of history could a greater command of the forces that shape history be achieved.

Thucydides remained a unique and lonely figure in Greece. He had no successor, though the following generations of Greek scholars and philosophers remained equally engrossed in the problem of the state. But the Greek philosophers of the fourth century looked at the state as an integral part of the natural order of the universe to be interpreted in terms of ultimate ends. Political science and history were broken apart, an event that still affects the division of our academic disciplines in spite of the disappearance of its original philosophical justification. A lowly place was assigned to history and Aristotle could say that poetry was something more philosophic and of graver import than history, since its statements were of the nature of universals, whereas those of history were singulars.

The Greek concept of history was the outgrowth of political experience and interest. This overwhelming motive at the same time, however, set definite limits to Greek history. The Greeks, and particularly an Ionian like Herodotus, possessed a lively curiosity about foreign cultures, but they never made a scientific effort to penetrate into the heart of a foreign civilization through languages and literature. Moreover, Greek ideas about history were formulated in a period in which the decline of the Greek states was already under way. This was clearly reflected in the notion of a cycle of history or even of a steady decline of history which formed a common theory of Greek historical thought.

While the Greek view of history was thus limited in scope it was also coupled with an interpretation of the role of the individual in society which arose out of the conditions of Greek historical existence. Greek rationalism had no organ for the free individual. The idea of the right of the individual to possess a sphere of his own was alien to the Greeks. The government was in total control of the community, and whatever freedom the individual might acquire he could gain only through participation in government. The Greek soul did not demand a field in life all to itself and beyond the social order. Slavery, disposal of newborn children, ostracism, etc., were symptoms of the low respect for the autonomy of the individual, and the extreme fierceness of the struggle of factions and classes for the control of the city government was a manifestation of the same philosophy of life.

Greek historical thought still advanced in one direction. Under the impression of Macedonian and Roman expansion and of the growing influence of the Orient, Polybius conceived of history as universal history. The national division and the monographic treatment of history were thus overcome. But his theory of the cycles of history and his study of the ideal forms of political constitutions as containing the key for an understanding of the rise and fall of states showed him as a true heir to the Greek tradition. The relationship of history and political science which he assumed is opposite to that of Thucydides. Polybius took the laws which had been developed by post-Aristotelian political science as the basis for an interpretation of history. Whereas to Thucydides political science was applied history, history becomes for Polybius applied political science.

Christian religion broke down the foundation on which Greek philosophy and science had been built. To the Greeks knowledge was the reflection of something existing objectively. In Christian religion truth originates with the inner experience of the individual, and the consciousness of the individual is a historical consciousness. Two central events, the creation and the appearance of Christ, determine Christian experience. History becomes the coordinated movement of mankind toward an ultimate goal. Creation, the advent of Christ, and final redemption are unique historic events. Consequently history does not repeat itself or move in cycles. The new vision of history was first expressed by St. Paul, who in his conscience experienced the conflict of Greek philosophy, Jewish law, and the faith in Christ in their deepest religious motivation. History was felt to be a universal process of the human soul.

This is not the place to analyze the Christian consciousness of history in all its far-reaching implications. Nor is there time to describe the actual growth of Christian historical thought through the next fifteen centuries. Undoubtedly the rich potentialities of the fundamental Christian concept of history were not exhausted by these ages, and the Hellenization and Latinization of Christian religion since the second century were largely responsible for the forms of medieval thought of history. Ancient and medieval Christianity did not produce a new critical history, probably not even exactly a new philosophy of history, but found its expression in a theology of history. History was the manifestation of God's providence. As such it had unity, but the ideal plan of history towered far above the earthly events which on the whole were mere appearances, in contrast to the divine omniscience and omnipotence. Apart from this theology of history, though, of course, very profoundly affected by it, the primitive forms of historiography like annals, chronicles, and legends lived on.

A renascence of Greek historical thought, chiefly through the medium of the Roman historians, took place in fifteenth-century Italy and reached its culmination in Machiavelli. It would not be correct to say that Thucydides stated his interpretation of politics in the terrifying Melian dialogue in which naked self-interest and the urge for power were exposed as the chief motives of human actions. In the general plan of Thucydides' work the Melian dialogue was to illustrate the degeneracy of Greek politics. A full understanding of Thucydidean ideas on the moving forces of political life requires a comparison with other speeches where the Greek historian showed the effect of reasonable virtues on history. Similarly, Machiavelli's teachings on power were counterbalanced by his insistence upon the constructive discipline of reason. He even discussed the problem of good and evil, which showed, to say the least, that he addressed himself to a Christian audience. Here, as in other instances, it is not difficult to prove Christian influences in Machiavelli. With these reservations in mind, however, it can be said that he renewed the political history and political science of Thucydides, Aristotle, and Polybius.

Broadly speaking, Machiavelli was closer to Thucydides than to Aristotle or even Polybius insofar as he endeavored to draw his lessons from realistic observations of actual historical events. The interest in the analysis of the constitutional forms of states stemmed, of course, from the Aristotelian tradition but was no longer expected to yield the ultimate answer in the quest for the causes of the growth and decline of states. Machiavelli—and incidentally Guicciardini as well—could say that the personal stature of the statesman was more important than monarchy and democracy. He expressed on his part the glorification of the strong and powerful individual so common in the age of the Italian Renaissance.

Thucydides had been an admirer of Pericles, but largely because Pericles was an ideal expression of the culture and society of Athens. Machiavelli viewed the great historic personality not so much as the child or representative of the community, but rather as its founder and independent manager. The great lawgivers of nations, like Moses or Solon, ranked highest in his estimation, since they had continued to rule their peoples far beyond their own generation through institutions of their creation. Statesmen were to Machiavelli great artificers using all forces of life, including religion, merely as means to achieve political control. The study of statecraft was the study of the techniques by which power could be gained and preserved. The political pragmatism of Greek history was thus revived, though with significant shifts of emphasis, which could be illustrated here only very sketchily. Together with it the belief in the repetitive or cyclical nature of the historical process returned.

Yet Machiavelli by himself was not the intellectual father of the modern state nor of modern history. The modern state, philosophically speaking, was the result both of the revival of the naturalistic concept of politics that originated with the Greeks and the Christian concept of history. It is true that the teachings of Machiavelli and his Italian successors facilitated the growth of the absolutistic state of the seventeenth and eighteenth centuries and stimulated its power politics to the point of endangering the great achievement of Western medieval history, the creation of an independent sphere of spiritual principles. Undoubtedly medieval man paid a high price for the relative autonomy of ideal values, since it tended to deprive natural life of its significance. On its part the absolutistic state of the late sixteenth and subsequent centuries began to use religion as a mere means to enhance the control of its subjects and to boost its power.

Yet the new absolutistic state of this age did not grow up in the Italy of Machiavelli, but in Spain, France, and England. As early as the Middle Ages Italy had had a history of her own. Nowhere in Europe had feudalism been as weak as in Italy, political division and lack of national coherence as marked. Against this historical background the political life of the city-states in the Renaissance must be seen. Machiavelli's political and historical theories and the political forms that were to dominate the times after his death originated in an entirely different setting. The national rulers of Western Europe were not usurpers but legitimate Christian kings and the protectors of the ancient customs of their peoples. It would be a grave historical error to identify arbitrary government and lawlessness with the emerging absolutistic monarchies of the Western European nations. On the contrary, in spite of many violent and revolutionary aberrations in the practices of absolutism, a keen sense of law and a live consciousness of the spiritual forces of history were preserved. And where political power became too oppressive, religious independence was reasserted, as in England, or a new "natural" religion was postulated as an idea above the political ethics of the ages. The tragic experiences of the confessional wars gave the movement toward a natural religion an irresistible momentum.

Thus history acquired a much broader interest and meaning in France from the days of Bodin to those of Montesquieu than it possessed in the strictly political interpretation of Machiavelli. Law was in the center of these studies, but religion and general civilization received almost equal attention. It was in this period, too, that those branches of study came into being without which a critical understanding of human life was impossible. Post-Aristotelian Greece had risen to the construction of the independent growth of arts and sciences but had never conceived of special histories of law, languages, and religions, nor of economics as a separate field of study. All of these helped to open new approaches to a deeper analysis of the social process and produced a passionate search for the facts of history which the Middle Ages had so greatly neglected. The magnificent works of Tillemont, Baronius, Muratori, and others have remained to the present day armories of historical knowledge.

The capacity for the reconstruction of the past led to the breakdown of the metaphysical concept of history. Following the model of Cartesian science historians were supposed to demonstrate the laws and mechanics of history. Moreover, the key to history was now to be found exclusively in the nature of man. Providence was dethroned, but even fate and fortune, which Thucydides as well as Machiavelli had considered to be the rulers of a substantial part of history, were excluded. Modern historiography looked for an explication of history in terms of human motives, interests, and thoughts.

But in spite of this secularization of thought the monopoly of political history was not revived. To the eighteenth century, history was history of civilization and even the most pronounced "political" historians of the nineteenth century, like Treitschke, tried to justify the dominant position which they assigned to the state not by mere reference to the role of power in history but to the cultural function of the state. In this respect the two centuries displayed the influence of a Christian heritage.

The Christian tradition, however, manifested itself even more clearly in the continuation of a teleological construction of history. The goal of history was variously defined. In Voltaire's case it was the enlightenment of the world by the growing strength of human reason. Hegel defined it as the consciousness of freedom through the realization of a deified state, Marx as the achievement of full freedom in a society liberated from the shackles of the state, while Comte found it in the full control of the social environment through the progress of technology and the science of society.

Among these three schools Hegel's philosophy of history represented a conscious and determined attempt at a synthesis of the Christian theology of history and the Greek concept of history. In his view historical knowledge was both the critical observation of historical phenomena and the inner experience of the human mind which arrive at the realization of the identity of the laws of history and those of human thinking. Philosophical logic and the logic of history conform and the dialectics of history is but the realization of the dialectics of the absolute mind.

The Historical School protested against the new metaphysical constructions of history as leading to rationalistic generalizations in which the true life of history would disappear. Savigny, Boeckh, Grimm, Ranke, and their successors emphasized the eternal mutation of history and the endless variety of its forms and causal relations. This led them to exclude from the study of history not only metaphysics but also pragmatism. The famous and so often misinterpreted statement from the preface of Ranke's first work, that he had only aimed at the reconstruction of past history as it actually happened (*wie es eigentlich gewesen sei*) was directed against the claim of Thucydides that through the reconstruction of real events the historian would also provide guidance for future generations. Thucydides believed in the practical immutability of history, Ranke in its variety.

The Historical School concentrated upon the revival of the past in its multifarious appearances, and during the last century historians have amassed a wealth of information about the history of mankind that no former age possessed. It is doubtful, however, whether they have exhausted the full meaning of the study of history. Count York, a friend of Wilhelm Dilthey and a philospher of history in his own right, once spoke of the "magic lantern" technique that, he asserted, Ranke was using. He thereby pointed his finger at one of the major weaknesses of modern historical writing. The mere visualization of the past is only a step, if the most important step, toward a critical understanding of history. By itself it tends to lead only to an aesthetic enjoyment of the colorful and multiform life of former ages or even to a sentimental nostalgia for things past.

But the historians of the nineteenth century, Ranke included, were not mere romantic visionaries. Most of them were convinced that they were mastering the world of history as realistically as the contemporary scientists were conquering the mysteries of nature. The historical method was construed as being analogous to the process of scientific inquiry. It was assumed that once the individual facts of history were properly verified and assembled they would yield the underlying pattern of universal history. Scientific investigation, however, does not proceed by mere observation. Science organizes its findings by mathematical or other principles of reasoning. Actually the historians, too, if they tried at all to fit the individual results of their specialized studies into a broad panorama of universal history, were in need of general ideas. Most of them borrowed them from the old philosophies of history or from the modern political creeds, which for their part had absorbed much of these philosophies.

The study of history and of nature cannot be construed as resting upon an identical methodology. Historical and scientific methods are as different as the physical and the human world. Wilhelm Dilthey was the first thinker to state the need for an independent theory of historical knowledge which alone would give historical scholarship a firm critical basis. He also saw that history had assumed a much more important place in human thinking as a consequence of the breakdown of the metaphysical philosophies which had claimed to be capable of defining the role of religion, of the state and society in absolute terms. The nineteenth century began to recognize that man and human institutions could be approached only through the study of their historical forms. But if this main thesis of the Historical School was correct —and as a matter of fact it has proved irresistible—mere visualization of these forms is not enough. It is necessary to analyze them with a view to the absolute potentialities of human life as such. Without this effort history would not preserve the deep motives of Western historical thought nor deserve a prominent place in modern education.

HISTORY AND
THE HUMANITIES*

THE ROLE OF modern science in the destruction of the metaphysical outlook of Western civilization and in the creation of modern rationalistic philosophies is universally acknowledged. The equally important part played in this process by the growth of modern historical thought is still far from being adequately appreciated. But Hume, Voltaire, and their successors by pronouncing the belief in history as a manifestation of the will of Providence a superstitious myth did exactly what the scientists were doing with regard to nature. As all magic forces were excluded from the analysis of the universe history was henceforth understood as the knowledge of human actions and thoughts.

Since the eighteenth century this has constituted the fundamental assumption in the study of history. In its origins it was closely allied with a faith in progress and the infinite perfectibility of man. Thus even in the secular philosophies of history produced in the eighteenth and early nineteenth centuries the teleological character of the old religious interpretation continued, and it has remained a most formidable influence in modern historical thinking. The new Jerusalem

* This paper was read at the Princeton Bicentennial Conference "The Humanistic Tradition in the Century Ahead," which took place October 16–18, 1946.

was envisaged in various forms. Voltaire conceived it as progress toward general enlightenment and happiness, Hegel as the consciousness of freedom through the realization of a deified state, Marx as the achievement of real freedom in the paradise of a classless, and consequently stateless, society. Even when Comte, Spencer, and others replaced the speculative philosophy of history by a "positive," and that meant scientific, study of history the teleological structure survived.

Against these philosophical and sociological ideas the Historical School rebelled. It originated in Germany, but soon found its representatives in every country. It was by no means confined to the study of politics but embraced languages and literature, law and economics as well. Nobody questions today that these historical studies produced greater and more reliable results than those of any older school. After a century of tireless endeavor our knowledge of history now extends over vast reaches of human civilization. If, however, our generation inquires into the general assumptions underlying the work of the students of history in the nineteenth century as stated by these students themselves, we find them, with few exceptions, espousing philosophies which do not stand up under critical review. With few exceptions we see them under the spell of the expanding natural sciences. In their opinion the task of historical research was the reconstruction of the past from the sources which, if purged of certain falsehoods, would tell the story of the past by themselves. A steady accumulation of purified sources would in due course overcome whatever subjectivity existed in the individual historian. Philosophy was to be excluded from the field of history, since it imposed an arbitrary pattern, alien to historical reality.

Though such ideas are still widely held in the historical profession, they have often enough been exposed as a naïve rationalization of the practice of the historical student, explicable by the intellectual climate of the last century and particularly by the inevitable conflict between the modern empirical study of history and the old speculative philosophy of history. This philosophy of history, though it contributed greatly to the modern awareness of history, was at the same time an impediment to the critical reconstruction of the historical world. The emphasis on detailed factual evidence and the exclusion of a teleological construction of history was a logical necessity. But these circumstances did not justify a divorce of history and philosophy. How dangerous such a separation might become was amply demonstrated whenever the empiristic historians attempted to present a view of general history. In that case they could be seen borrowing heavily from the old philosophies of history which they themselves decried or, even worse, they were swayed by the naturalistic and materialistic ideologies of modern nationalism.

The study of history would inevitably lose any sense of direction and could not claim to yield objective and valid knowledge if its methods and aims were not lifted into clear consciousness and made the object of critical analysis. Philosophy and history are closely joined together, though their relationship is of an entirely different nature from that visualized in the eighteenth century. Philosophy cannot determine the contents of history by mere speculation. Philosophy is as dependent on history as it is on science. When Kant wrote his *Critique of Pure Reason* he described the methods employed by the natural sciences. A critique of historical reason which Wilhelm Dilthey first postulated and to which a large number of scholars of the last and present generation have turned their attention would have to start in similar manner from the scrutiny of historical methodology.

But it is not only the epistemological concern which brings philosophy and history together. It is the fundamental problem of philosophy itself, the question "What is man?" which compels the philosopher to study history. For the subjective nature of man can be approached only through history. There is no new beginning in life. My every action and thought presupposes and contains an earlier background of thought and action. And what is true of individuals applies equally to civilizations or world history. In this sense, Ortega y Gassett could recently say that "man has no nature, but only history."[1]

Such a statement is based on the recognition that historical time is something entirely different from time as it appears in nature. Any natural phenomenon takes place in time. But whether or not one uses words like history of nature, history of the universe, etc., it is evident, for example, that the chain reaction of an atomic bomb explosion, though it constitutes a sequence of events in time, is not *per se* a historical event. The historical significance of Los Alamos, Hiroshima, and Nagasaki rests in the growth of the modern scientific mind, in the reasons which induced the American government to support the scientific and technological development of atomic energy and to employ it as a weapon in the final phase of the War. This is not the time to list all possible aspects of the invention of atomic energy that historians will have to treat. Suffice it to say that all of them will be subjects to be defined in terms of human motives, actions, and reactions. For that reason they are unique events which will not repeat themselves, in contrast to the natural chain-reaction of an atomic explosion which will happen in the same form according to the same laws of nature whenever the same elements meet under the same circumstances.

The history of man, therefore, implies more than mere change in time. Historical time is meaningful time, made meaningful by singular human actions. The repetitious appetites and desires of man's physical being are not a subject of historical study. But, for example, the growth of specific forms of courtship and love in human civilization is a legitimate subject of historical inquiry. In addition to the principle of continuity history is determined by the principle of individuation. This process of individuation has most often been explained in a more or less Hegelian vein as the manifestation of reason. However, man always remains tied to his physical nature and human consciousness expresses not only reasoning thought, but will power and feeling as well. The historian will not expect history ever to reach a final goal beyond which human nature would be moved only by reason, or history would change into eternity.

The historian as a historian cannot even predict the outlines of the age immediately ahead with any claim to pronounce a valid judgment, since it would conflict with his basic premises and findings. History has neither a new beginning nor a final ending. It can only be conceived as the realization of the potentialities of man in historic time. But historical study, by retracing the struggle of man for the control of nature and by reviving the thoughts and conscious life of the past, offers the living generation the challenge to make its own vital decisions on the basis of a critical knowledge of the full scope of former human experiences and achievements. It thus enables the individual human being to expand his experience beyond his actual station in life or a historic society to absorb the fruits of events in which it had no part itself. The study of history opens the road to participation in the fullness of human civilization.

This participation has to be understood literally. Whereas the natural scientist perceives phenomena which have a reality independent from the observer history is only real in the consciousness of the historian. There is great significance in the fact, so annoying to many historians, that the word "history" means both history as actuality (*res gestae*) and written history. The past is present only as far as it is relived by the historian through sympathy and understanding. The central problems of a historical methodology or epistemology hinge upon the fact that an objective knowledge of the past can only be attained through the subjective experience of the scholar.

The study of history offers no escape from historicity and all the limitations of historic man apply to the individual student of history. As a matter of fact, without subjectivity we could not even hope to penetrate into history. Historians should keep their feet firmly planted in the life of their own age and participate bravely in its labors. They will not thereby gain answers to the problems of history, but they will be able to formulate questions with which to approach the past. And history gives answers only to those who know how to ask questions. Still, this is just the beginning of historical inquiry. The process of historical verification and understanding is a continuous struggle to move from a subjective toward a universal position, from a captivity in the floating and fortuitous moment of history, called the present, to a share in the objective human experiences as manifested in the historic civilizations.

The critical character of historical interpretation is ultimately determined by the underlying concept of man, which is not merely the result of a reading in the past but also of a simultaneous self-analysis of the observer. In this critical revival of the past the living generation achieves a higher consciousness of its own being. Therefore, historical study is a humanistic endeavor. Beginning with Cicero all the humanists desired to know the greatness and range of human nature and were animated by the faith that such knowledge would endow them with a greater capacity for the realization of the highest ideals in their own time. Modern historical study stands in this tradition, though it has changed almost all other ideas and methods of the humanism of former centuries. Today history is the approach to the knowledge of man and through history we acquire the wealth of former civilizations. The critical awareness of the potentialities of man enables us to act in our own time with higher insight and vigor.

THE SCIENCE OF HISTORY*

THERE HAS BEEN much complaint of the slight interest that the public, even the educated public, has shown in historical research. The students of history look with some envy at the natural sciences which enjoy general public acclaim because of their obvious usefulness to society. The natural sciences offer definite results and valid truths. The whole organization of our daily life proves the gigantic progress that the human mind has made in mastering nature. High hopes have been entertained that the expansion of the natural sciences would ultimately place the well-being of the human race on a safe and objective basis. These expectations have been cruelly shattered by the experiences of the last years. Technology does not merely improve the efficiency of peacetime organization, but of war organization as well. The gruesome story of the destruction wrought by modern arms is as much a result of the progress of natural sciences as the millions of jobs created by their inventiveness.

It would be as serious a mistake to blame the terrors of our age upon the natural sciences as it was to expect from them the solution of the issues which have been and will forever remain human and moral problems. The natural

* This essay formed part of a Princeton symposium on the interpretation of History, 1940.

sciences are dealing with means and not with ends. They have in fact made one great contribution to general education. They have freed man from superstitious beliefs in nature. By demonstrating that the process of nature can be explained by laws of reason they have given courage to all those who endeavor to expand the power of the human mind into all fields of life. But a concrete program of social and individual life is beyond the realm of the natural sciences.

If we turn our attention to the part played by historical thought in modern history we may feel even more disappointed. A philosopher recently asked whether the battle raging in Russia—the greatest battle in history in terms of number of men and extension of battlefield—was not actually a conflict between the left and right wing of Hegel's school. Without doubt ideological wars are to a very large extent traceable to diversions of historical thought which thus acts as a destructive rather than liberating force. In the growth of modern nationalism the influence of the teaching of history is of primary significance and has done much to foment the bellicose instincts of men.

But the critical historian will say that this is not history, but human passions, myth and interests costuming themselves in historical dress. He will maintain that at least the science of history is above the heat of battle. This does not mean that he himself as an individual has entered a realm of calm objectivity. But he trusts that the ideal of a science of history can be made evident by a common effort of scholars, and that the science of history is one of the strongest forces in the defense of civilization as such. Moreover, he would state his belief that critical historical research has produced results which are as valid and useful as the conclusions of natural sciences. This is the point of view we are taking when we talk of a science of history. Great confusion surrounds the term. Different people have understood it differently. They have postulated full identity of method in natural and historical studies. History is supposed to yield laws by which the whole historical process can be classified. But such a definition of the science of history is nothing but a reflection of the exaggerated significance which was at times assigned to the natural sciences outside their own field. To talk about a science of history means nothing but an affirmation of the critical and systematic approach to history, and the validity of the results achieved in this way.

To understand the science of history we are well advised if we turn to those who created it and brought it to highest perfection. Two men seem to me to tower above all other historians: Thucydides and Ranke. The first of these was an active statesman and soldier who had to live through the greatest catastrophe that imagination could conceive. The second, a scholar and teacher by profession, was born amidst the turmoil of the World War that followed in the wake of the French Revolution. In contrast to Thucydides, Ranke saw the pattern of the old Europe emerge again, if considerably modified, and the continuity of historical development restored. Both represent the greatest progress made in their age toward a critical study of history, and modern historical research and writing still rest on the foundations which they have laid.

Certain ideas or images of past and future constitute a basic element of any civilization, and all of them show a certain historical consciousness. But, of the twenty-odd civilizations which we know, only a few have given historical thought the prominent place in life that it assumed in the ancient world and its affiliated civilization, the Western world. Historical thought has been one of the mainsprings of action and contemplation in the history of Western man. Moreover, only in ancient and Western civilization did historical consciousness grow beyond the primitive stage of mythological interpretation, or even beyond the next two stages of the human interest story on one side, and the factual state chronicle on the other. These three types of history writing we can find in a good many civilizations. We meet them in the Old Testament where mythological interpretation appears side by side with the chronicles of kings and the novelistic treatment of episodes of the past in the stories of David, Absalom, etc. The same forms of historical writing can be found in other civilizations, in the first place in Greece. The Greeks, however, went one step further by trying to replace the mythological and poetic by a scientific interpretation of history. At the same time when, in Ionian civilization, the science of nature superseded the old cosmology, the memorable attempt was made to explain history without reference to the miraculous and legendary, and to find its explanation in the immanent qualities of human life. It was Thucydides who defined the task of the new history.

"On the one hand I have given no greater credence to the accounts turned into song by poets adorning and amplifying their theme than I have on the other hand to the chroniclers who composed with a view rather of pleasing the ear than of telling the truth, since their stories cannot be tested, and most of them have from lapse of time so won their way into the region of the fabulous as to be incredible. . . . As to the facts of the occurrences of the war, I have thought it my duty to give them, not as ascertained from any chance informant nor as seemed to me probable, but only after investigating with the greatest possible accuracy each detail. . . . And it may well be that the absence of the fabulous from my narrative will seem less pleasing to the ear; but whoever shall wish to have a clear view both of the events which have happened and of those which will some day, in all human probability, happen again in the same or a similar way—for these to adjudge my history useful will be enough for me. And, indeed, it has been composed, not as a prize essay to be heard for the moment, but as a possession for all time."

The twenty-second chapter of Thucydides, from which this quotation has been chosen, was the first program of a science of history. The legendary and fabulous were banned from the realm of historical study, and accurate truth, achieved by critical analysis of contemporary sources, became the exclusive aim of historical research. Rhetorical or literary brilliance for its own sake was also excluded, but "usefulness" in a philosophical sense was proclaimed the highest criterion. When Thucydides proudly stated that his work was designed as an "everlasting possession" he wished to express his belief that it enshrined truth as objectively valid and useful as the results of any other branch of science.

Critical methods for the gathering of historical evidence did not in themselves raise historical studies to the rank of a science. Otherwise Thucydides would have written annals or a series of important incidents of the Peloponnesian War. But to Thucydides the truthful reconstruction of the past was the means for opening up a view on the general causes and motives of human action. Thucydides expresses this ultimate goal of his history by using a literary device which modern historians could not imitate. In his work the protagonists of the historical drama give speeches reflecting on the profound issues of the war. He has been harshly criticized by modern scholars for inserting idealized or fictitious speeches. But since he himself states that these speeches were not authentic in the literal sense, he could hardly be accused of forgery. A careful study of the speeches would show that they contain a great element of realistic truth, and beyond that reflections which are not essentially different from the observations that a modern writer would add to his descriptive narrative. Modern historians were tutored in literary expression by the prose writers of the eighteenth and nineteenth centuries, Thucydides by the Athenian poets and sophists. He was, therefore, likely to personify the different aspects of the truth, as in the Greek dialogue, or as in the comments of the chorus in the Athenian tragedy where the light of the truth is broken into its component colors by a number of persons presenting different views.

The deeper meaning of Thucydides' speeches becomes evident in an examination of their place in the work as a whole.

The touch of genius appears in the device by which Athens is first characterized by its enemies. From the speech of the Corinthian minister in Sparta the reader learns for the first time how the neighbors of Athens felt the pressure of her might and the threat of her political cunning. But through accusations and detractions the reader begins at the same time to realize some of the greatness of the Athenian commonwealth. In subsequent chapters new glimpses are afforded, culminating in the Funeral Speech of Pericles in which the essence of Athenian democracy is fully illuminated.

Such methods were in line with the literary taste of the age, but Thucydides did not use them for mere adornment. Even in this respect his aim was not the beautiful, but the useful or, as we may say now, science rather than literature. The underlying issues of the war are characterized from different angles and so thrown into full relief. The pattern of human life, as the philosophical mind of Thucydides sees it, becomes apparent through the deliberate use of these various perspectives, and for this reason the speeches are essential means to express the historian's intent. To the son of the Greek *polis* man is a political being and history is accordingly political history. The currency in which the great changes of history are registered is power and force. The Peloponnesian War was inevitable with the growth of Athenian might in which the other Greek states were bound to find a vital danger to their own freedom. Moral guilt has no meaning in judging historical catastrophes, since they occur by force of nature.

There exists, however, for Thucydides another level of human life. In treating the decisive turning point of the war, the failure of the Sicilian expedition, he indicates that the strategy of the conquest of Sicily was sound. The plan miscarried because of the fall of Alcibiades. When he was banned from Athens the only statesman who could have directed the execution of the scheme with hope of success was expelled from active leadership. Thucydides does not doubt that Alcibiades invited violent criticism by his personal conduct. The intel-

lectual qualities of a political leader were coupled with frivo-
lous passions. Thus he unsettled the balance of forces on
which the Athenian state had rested. Passions were the motives of human action, but they could be moderated and led
into the right direction by reason and wisdom. Athens had
achieved such leadership in figures like Pericles. A similar
equipoise had existed in communal life as well. Athenian government, culture, arts, and sciences were the result of a high
vitality tempered by wisdom. But in Alcibiades private passions and public virtues were in conflict, and consequently
the passions of the mass could triumph over prudent leadership. His fall was the prologue to the rule of the demagogue.

Moral forces play a part in human history insofar as the
education of a nation and its leadership determine policies.
This interpretation shows Thucydides as a student of contemporary Greek philosophy and science. His concept of man,
his ideas about passion and reason bear the impress of the
scientific speculation of his day. From here stems what is
usually called his "objectivity." In his treatment he takes a
standpoint far above the struggling factions of the day. He
finds an explanation of causes, motives, and results by relating them to what he conceives to be the profoundest conception of human life. This enables him to lend life and color to
friend and enemy alike. His own role during the war becomes
incidental, just a welcome opportunity to gather material and
to gain a more realistic understanding of the events of the war.
The historian has forgotten his earthly station by ascending
to the heights of humanity to which Greek philosophy and
education had opened a path.

There is an individual pride in Thucydides, which was
closely connected with another idea of his history. In the
Funeral Speech of Pericles Athenian civilization is described
as the highest form of culture to which the Greeks had risen.
For Thucydides its ideals were not invalidated by the political
catastrophe of 404 B.C. He had seen them lowered by the
Athenians themselves and later brought down by their ene-

mies, but his faith that no higher human achievement existed, that they were also "useful" for all time, was not shaken. In the Athenian philosophy he found the most logical system of explanation of human life. By adapting it to history and illuminating the tragic cataclysm of the Peloponnesian War he wanted to testify to the everlasting quality of the scientific mind.

The critical analysis of sources and the reconstruction of individual scenes of the past was to Thucydides but a *methodos* and this means a way to something. As a doctor would be unable to determine the state of health without a careful examination of the symptoms of a disease, thus the diagnostician of historical life has first to verify the phenomena in which this life demonstrates its reality. But the goal of the study of history is to understand past events and conditions as the logical outcome of human nature and of its place in the world. As far as an historian is unable to transcend the limitations of his own private experiences he is inclined to identify human nature with his own self. Critical participation in the general knowledge of a civilization provides him with guiding stars for a more than subjective understanding of history. The wealth of the scientific and philosophical ideas of Ionia and Athens contributed to the range of Thucydides' vision. In choosing his position in the intellectual discussion of his age he was enabled to proceed from the actual events to the human sources of action.

This was the beginning of the science of history and for two thousand years the critical approach of Thucydides was not matched by any historian. This does not mean that there were no other great historians; in fact, even some of his predecessors could be placed above him in certain respects. Herodotus surpassed him in his interest in universal history, which, after two centuries, was revived by Polybius to become later the basis of all Christian historiography. Herodotus was not only more universal, but also more catholic in his studies. In contrast to the political history of Thucydides, monographically

written, Herodotus' history is of universal scope, and deals
with folklore, culture, and religion as well as politics. But
Herodotus was not able to avoid the pitfalls of such universal
curiosity. The logical unity of his work suffered.

In turning from Thucydides to Leopold Ranke we should
again not forget his precursors. The old commonplace statement that the eighteenth century was unhistorical has long
been discarded. The eighteenth century was one of the greatest centuries of historical thought. Nor did progress cease
with Ranke. But there can be no doubt that in him historical
consciousness reached a new height of maturity, and that in
the enormous range of his works and teaching no modern historian has equaled him. He himself stated: "We have great
teachers not in order to stick to their words and to repeat
them; it is only the spirit who vivifies in science as elsewhere."[1] This spirit wrestled with the fundamental problems
of the science of history during a long life.

From his ninetieth year the following remark of Ranke on
the origins of his first work has come to us: "In the twenties
of the nineteenth century the conviction spread that only a
deeper study of the foundations of states and empires would
satisfy the needs of the future. The romantic historical writings of Walter Scott . . . contributed chiefly to awaken an interest in the actions and attitudes of past ages. I was myself
sufficiently attracted by them and I read more than one of
these works with lively interest, but I was also offended by
them. Among other things I was hurt by the way in which
Charles the Bold and Louis XI were treated in his *Quentin
Durward,* in full contradiction to the historical sources, even
in the details. I studied Commines and the contemporary reports . . . and gained the conviction that Charles the Bold
and Louis XI, as Scott depicts them had never existed. The
good and learned author probably knew that himself. But I
felt unable to pardon him for adding traits to his treatment
which were entirely unhistorical and for presenting them
as if he believed them. In comparing the two I gained the

conviction that the historical reports themselves were more beautiful and, in any case, more interesting than the romantic fiction. Thereafter, I turned away from it altogether and decided to avoid everything fictitious and fanciful and to cling strictly to the facts."[2]

The parallelism with Thucydides is close, and in fact Ranke himself often confessed that he learned more from Thucydides than from any other historian. The programmatic preface with which he accompanied his first work in the year 1824 makes this influence quite clear, indicating at the same time the new direction which he gave to historical studies. His first book was entitled *Histories of the Latin and German Nations, from 1494–1514.* In the introduction he explained that neither the old concept of a universal Christendom, nor that of Europe as such, nor even that of a Latin Christianity could logically be used as a framework of modern history. Only by studying the Latin and Germanic nations together could he find the unity that underlay all modern history. Their growth showed a common pattern and a continuous exchange of ideas affecting their lives. Their unity in peace and war seemed to Ranke the true theme of modern history, and he proposed to prove their close community by the study of their life on the eve of their greatest division, just before the Reformation.

The insistence upon the inherent unity of the subject is in principle very similar to Thucydides' demonstration of the common history of the Hellenic states and its tragic culmination in the Peloponnesian War. And again he seems partly to point back to Thucydides in the following famous remarks: "History has had assigned to it the task of judging the past, of instructing the present for the benefit of the ages to come. The present study does not assume such a high office; it only wants to show *wie es eigentlich gewesen.*" The literal translation would be: "It only wants to show what actually occurred." But a more correct rendering would be: "It wants merely to reconstruct the actual past." After this statement

Ranke moves even closer to Thucydides. Only contemporary sources, critically sifted and cross-examined could form the basis of research, and then he goes on to say:

"Out of the subject and the material comes the form. You could not expect from history the same free treatment of its subject which is looked for, at least in theory, in a work of literature, and I do not know if those are right who find this in the works of Greek and Roman masters. Strict presentation of the facts, conditional and unattractive though they may be, is unquestionably the supreme law. Next seems to me to come the presentation of the unity and of the progress of events. Instead of starting with a general description of the political institutions of Europe, which would perhaps have confused and certainly have diverted attention, I have preferred to describe each nation, each power, each individual more extensively only at the time when it assumes an active or leading part."[3]

A unified subject, critical study of sources, accuracy of presentation, and an organization of the narrative in which each stage appears as the logical result of the earlier events and in which all historical forces are strictly subordinated to the general development—these are the chief maxims of Ranke's history. The difference between Ranke and Thucydides seems almost negligible. But two points deserve special consideration.

What did Ranke have in mind when he declined to act as a judge of the past? To Thucydides, as we have seen, the moral judgment was not a genuine historical judgment, either. Historical events were to him symptoms of growth. He comes sometimes close to an organic or biological interpretation, most clearly in the chapters in which he describes the transformation of the human mind under the impact of the war in terms of a medical history or a feverish illness. Thucydides underlines this viewpoint by turning immediately thereafter to the history of the plague in Athens, from the pathology of history to pure pathology. Historical events are analyzed by

him with cold anatomy. The ideal values are far above the
sufferings of mortal men, no ray from the stars is able to melt
the heart of the goddess of fate, *Tyche,* who holds men bound
by her austere laws.

Ranke's Christian consciousness made such an interpretation impossible. Christian religion had brought heaven and
earth closer together. The individual was able to overcome
Tyche and to experience the reality of metaphysical and
moral values in his own life. Whether or not such an approach
was logically bound to result in a theology of history is doubtful; in any event it made it impossible to look at individuals
merely as fodder for the mills of historical fate, or at best as
types and symbols of groups and ages. Obviously the individual was now to be judged in terms of both his actions and his
intentions as well, how far he achieved Christian perfection.
The same applied to generations and periods.

Ranke did not question the Christian attitude. He never
entertained any doubt that the individual had a destiny apart
from his participation in the historical process. Moreover, he
knew that moral and ideal forces had a direct bearing on the
course of historical events and that the struggle between them
and the stubborn reality of matter took place in the life of the
individual. He was, therefore, tremendously interested in biography and fathered the idea of a German National Biography (*Allgemeine Deutsche Biographie*), a work which
served as a model for similar undertakings in other countries.
But he considered biography as a mere auxiliary branch of
historical science. He himself wrote no true biography. His
monograph on Wallenstein he called a *History* of Wallenstein,
his book on Hardenberg, *Hardenberg and the History of the
Prussian State.* There are two small biographical articles in the
fifty-four volumes of his collected works, both of them in an-
nexes to other writings, and both of them dealing with what
he considered pathological cases, namely the two "digres-
sions" on Don Carlos and on Queen Christina. As a rule the
individual appears in Ranke's histories at such moments when

he appears in "an active or leading role" of general history. In each case Ranke takes great pains to delineate the individual carefully and to determine his original contribution to the event, but he refuses to act as a moral judge.

As far as we can see Ranke's treatment of the individual was motivated by various considerations. The first was chiefly critical. The historian, he said, sees into the face of persons of the past, but he is unable to see into their hearts. He felt that the depth of personal life was unfathomable by critical reason and reached into a realm that preceded and transcended history. From this Ranke concluded that the individual was a legitimate subject of study only as far as his impact on the course of general history could be verified and known. With these assumptions it would be illogical to assign to history the task of passing moral judgment upon individuals. The historian has to understand and record, as Ranke once put it, "the origins and forms of all the actions and sufferings of this creature, at the same time wild, fierce, and reckless, and good, noble, and calm, of this contaminated and pure being, which we are ourselves."[4] But the historian has to understand these actions as manifestations of human nature as it unfolds in the world of time.

Here a second line of thought becomes visible, and this is the one which leads farthest beyond Thucydides. Thucydides believed in the unalterable character of man. By a monographic treatment of history he felt certain that he could grasp the meaning of human actions, not merely in the period under review, but for all time to come. What some modern historians consider to be the very essence of historicity, namely the notion of the uniqueness of all forms of historical life, was entirely lacking in Thucydides. Ranke's emphasis upon the uniqueness of the individual or of an individual period of history has profoundly influenced such a definition. Meinecke's great work on the origins of modern *Historismus* seems to me to suffer somewhat from this narrow definition of historicity.

When Ranke refused "to instruct the present for the benefit of ages to come" and reduced his study "to the reconstruction of the actual past" he took issue, of course, with Thucydides' pragmatic view of history. To Ranke there was no repetition in history, either in individuals, or in situations and ages. Therefore no recurrence of the past was to be expected in the future. This would have confined the task of reconstructing the past to a visual operation. "History wants merely to see and to understand in order to report what it sees," we read in the introduction to Ranke's second book on *The Serbian Revolution* of 1829, a book that Niebuhr called the greatest book on contemporary history which he knew. But Ranke's general attitude to history and politics is not adequately described in such statements. They were largely polemic remarks made against that type of philosophy of history which was represented by Voltaire and the Enlightenment, and had found a modified expression in Hegel's teachings. These philosophies of history postulated a predetermined goal of history and maintained that all individual events were only illustrations of one and the same scheme of historical evolution.

Ranke's and his successors' objections against this type of philosophy of history has unfortunately induced historians and philosophers to assume a logical incompatibility of philosophy and history altogether, an entirely arbitrary exaggeration most harmful to the growth of our studies. Ranke restored the critical method of historical research so much neglected, or even disregarded, by the philosophers of history of the Voltaire and Hegel school. In this he was clearly influenced by the model of natural sciences and their inductive method. But this was not yet history to him. History was not merely to be visualized, but to be understood, and it could be understood only in reference to the totality of the historical process.

In connection with the discussion of the problem of historical versus biographical treatment we have already noticed Ranke's anxiety to secure unity in his study of an historical subject, and we have seen that he found this unity in the "progress of events." He conceived of history as a unified process, not as a conglomeration of various fields of study to be cultivated by the same method. The monographic approach was to him only a preparation to universal history. Although he resented the attempts of certain philosophers to formulate *a priori* laws of universal history, the conception of a universal history itself was in his mind from his early days and gained clearer shape as his studies progressed. He saw individual forces in history everywhere, but he recognized in them the manifestation of a general ideal power. There is no history, but only the life of animals, as long as the mind is not accentuating human actions and producing individual forms of life. This interaction between the mind and nature is the universal principle to be used by the historian. The concept of uniqueness found its counterpart in that of universality.

In one of the last volumes of his Universal History written shortly before his death he described his position in this manner: "Apart from and beyond the histories of individual nations I assume a specific principle of universal history: it is the principle of a common life of the human race which dominates the nations without resolving itself in them. One could call it culture, preservation and expansion of civilization, not of culture alone, as it is usually understood, which would narrow down the horizon to sciences and arts. Civilization comprises at the same time religion and state, the free development of all these forces looking toward the ideal. Civilization forms the foremost acquisition and possession of humanity handed on and augmented from generation to generation . . . it is inseparably bound together with politics and war and with all the events which constitute the facts of history. The idea of universal history does not appear in generally valid forms, but in a variety of forms according to the special life of the nations and not at all in peaceful and undisturbed development but the continuous conflict and struggle; for to quarrel is the nature of man."

This was the answer of the mature scholar Ranke. History had become to him, instead of the critical and optical exploration of isolated subjects, the critically enlightened awareness of human civilization in its totality. Thucydides could not have stated the task of the historian in this form. Ranke, by summarizing experiences of the Christian era, was in fact the fulfillment of Herodotus as well as of Thucydides, giving to historical studies the broadest vision and the power to implement that vision at a moment when the history of Western civilization became world history.

The reason for recalling the two greatest historical writers has been to show the birth of historical science. We should not dogmatize on their work. I have left out apsects of Ranke's work which were less of an achievement. It should be admitted that his abstention from judgments was not always the result of a higher wisdom but a desire to avoid controversial topics. His own political views deserve less criticism than they have usually found. Very few of his works are really marred by such biases, and in some of his writings on contemporary history he has shown an insight which should still make them preferred reading for modern students of history. But it is probably correct to say that the experience of the restoration of the old powers and ideas after the revolutionary and Napoleonic wars made him exaggerate the continuity and even the validity of the old forces. At times he went so far as to become an advocate of the political *status quo,* presenting his views as a result of historical research. The statesman-scholar Thucydides, under the impression of defeat, did not mix with the politics of his day; the professor was not to the same degree shaken out of his personal aspirations.

But all these questions are of minor significance for our problem. No individual could ever hope to identify his own position with the idea of science itself. This, however, does not prove science to be an illusion. We have seen the intellectual experiences which set Thucydides and Ranke on the road to historical truth. Both chose the critical method so closely akin to the natural sciences, or to Hippocrates in one case and to Descartes in the other. But the critical method by itself would not have made them historians. Their concept of history was the result of a general examination of the objective results of their own civilization, and this meant a critical participation in the discussion of human nature. The concept of history and the philosophical concept of man are inseparably bound together, and no scientific history is possible without the free study of both these problems. Wherever the concept of man is merely the reflection of human passion, the science of history ceases to exist.

It is on this level that philosophy and history come together. They are joined together by their common effort to understand man. History describes him in his concrete variety and unity in time. To do it critically and scientifically, the student of history has to overcome the subjectivity of his initial position. This implies a reorientation and self-analysis which can find its direction only by an active participation in the fundamental intellectual efforts of the age. For history is the critical consciousness of civilization about its own past. As such, it can claim a decisive part in general education, but it can maintain its critical vigor only by preserving its universal outlook in exchange with other branches of knowledge. Our historical studies would become saltless if they ceased to feel themselves in the midst of the Humanities. The significant function of history is to remind men of the role of human nature in time and history through a progressive understanding of the processes of human civilization. This perspective is at the same time a moral postulate: to maintain the dignity of man and his heritage of civilization.

JACOB BURCKHARDT
AS HISTORICAL THINKER*

AMONG THE SCHOLARS who in the course of the nineteenth century created a new intimate relationship between modern men and history the Swiss Jacob Burckhardt occupied a peculiar place of his own. He stood outside the line of the philosophers of history, like Hegel and Schelling, or Comte and Mill. At the same time, though a practicing historian, he held aloof from the schools of political history, which dominated historical studies practically everywhere during his lifetime. He made himself known as a master of the history of culture, *Kulturgeschichte,* an approach to history that has nothing to do with what is called history of culture in present-day America under the influence of modern anthropology. But Burckhardt's *Kulturgeschichte* was also quite different from the old tradition of history of civilization that stemmed largely from Voltaire's *histoire des moeurs* and found its best-known German representatives in Burckhardt's lifetime in W. H. Riehl and Gustav Freytag. Actually Burckhardt developed his own type of *Kulturgeschichte* that in spite of its neglect of the narration of political events was deeply concerned with politics. Moreover, although Burckhardt's historical works may appear to the casual reader as the works of an aesthetic and literary personality rather than of a scientific, let alone sys-

* A fragment.

tematic philosophical mind, there was behind them not only a well-thought-out methodology but also a profound desire to derive from history definite answers to the vital problems of human life. All the writings which were published after his death revealed with growing clarity the philosophical intent of Burckhardt's artful historical scholarship. He was not seeking a philosophy of history in the usual sense nor a concrete program of political action, but rather a philosophy of life grounded upon the contemplation of human history. As he once said with regard to the political pragmatists: "We do not study history to be clever for the next day but to become wise forever." But this wisdom was of another type than that presented by the older or contemporary philosophers of history.

I

But before exploring the character and method of Burckhardt's thought on history it may be useful to describe quite briefly his outward life, his works, and his inner development. Burckhardt, born in 1818, came from a long line of Basel ministers. His father was the preacher at Basel's ecclesiastical center and proudest historic monument, the Muenster, founded by the German emperor Henry II and built on a hill that had been first fortified by the Romans. Except for few years of his life Jacob Burckhardt remained close to the Basel Muensterberg. The University, whose most famous professor he was to become, was quite close to the cathedral and when he looked out from the window of his lecture hall the same vista would open as from the cathedral square. Down at the foot of the escarpment the Rhine, still young and untamed, rushed by under the Gothic bridge; beyond, straight north, the hills and mountains of the Black Forest formed a dramatic panorama while to the northwest the open Rhine valley drew the observers' eyes to far-off distances. This magnificently molded landscape had been the scene of continuous

historical changes. Burckhardt's father had still seen the
Breisgau under Austrian rule and Alsatia under many different political authorities. Then the French Revolution and Napoleon had upset old traditional institutions, including the ancient state of Switzerland. The Restoration did not restore
the old order but brought a pacification which re-established
some historical continuity. Still, the tremor over the momen-
tous political upheaval did not quite vanish.

The Basel Muenster was, however, not a mere landmark
and guide to the history of the surrounding region, but it was
itself a historic work of art. The zealous iconoclasm of the
Swiss Reformers had deprived its interior of all its artistic
sculpture and paintings. The student of architecture may not
be entirely ungrateful for such despoliation, for the beautiful
proportions and the dimensions of the structure can be more
easily enjoyed. But the intimate thoughts of generations of
worshipers were blotted out, though perhaps not altogether.
Some medieval sculpture was left on the outside of the cathedral. The great rose window at the front was treated by the
medieval artists as a wheel of fortune. It was meant to depict that interpretation of secular history which had lingered
on through the Middle Ages in spite of the official Augustinian theology of history. Blind Fortune turning her wheel
might enable ambitious men clinging to the wheel to rise to
the zenith of power, but irrespective of any personal achievement and merit they would be carried down again by the
same movement. While the medieval rose window thus symbol-
ized the vanity and fickleness of worldly success the grave of
the great Erasmus, whom Burckhardt's liberal colleagues
used to portray as an optimistic rationalist, showed that sixteenth-century humanism had not given up to worry over the
transcendental world. The tombstone inside the Muenster displayed the god whom Erasmus from his early days had held
before himself, Terminus, the warner of death.

The few illustrations must suffice to give an idea of how
Basel contributed to endow Burckhardt with an early aware-

ness of historical subjects. On the other hand he parted from other influences that surrounded his youth. After two years of theological study he decided to give up every attempt to follow his father's career and to study history and history of art instead. In the fall of 1839 he left Basel for the Prussian capital Berlin, then the Mecca of historians. The young Swiss disliked the capital of Prussia but found his boldest expectations for historical scholarship far surpassed by what he found. Soon he admitted that all he had known about historical studies had been as superficial as mere "hearsay" knowledge, "now I have met history in titanic greatness." Four professors were of this titanic quality: Franz Kugler, J. G. Droysen, August Boeckh, and Leopold Ranke. In a quantitative way Jacob Burckhardt learned most from Kugler, the professor of the history of art. Moreover, the amiable and interesting Kugler, only ten years older than the young Swiss student, became not only the teacher of Burckhardt in all the professional matters of the history of art but also a close friend to his early death in the fifties.

Johann Gustav Droysen was then in his most productive period. The Prussian state whose chief laudatory historian he was to become together with Treitschke after 1850 did not pay him any stipend for his lectures in ancient history. As a consequence Droysen taught twenty hours at a Berlin high school apart from his eight hours at the university. In those same years Droysen produced not only his *Alexander the Great*, but also his history of Hellenism, through which he first envisaged and named this age of history, as Burckhardt did twenty years later with the age of the Renaissance. Droysen, among others a friend of Felix Mendelssohn-Bartholdy and incidentally the creator of the best German translation of Aristophanes, was a man of wide aesthetic interests and also among all the German nineteenth-century historians the one most deeply engrossed in the study of the philosophical foundations of historical knowledge. But as far as can be judged, Droysen was chiefly important for Burckhardt's scholarly growth by introducing the future historian of Constantine the Great to the history of Hellenism.

In August Boeckh, Burckhardt met a true representative of the Goethe-Humboldt generation who had been a professor in Berlin University since its foundation in 1810. Boeckh was the greatest German scholar of classics in the first half of the nineteenth century, equally at home in classic literature and the *realia* of ancient life. It was his life-dream to write a comprehensive work on Greek civilization, which he planned to call *Hellen*. Only parts of this plan he completed, since he was drawn more and more into the critical editing of new historical sources. His *Inscriptiones Graecae* are his main monument in this field of learned endeavor that formed at the same time the bridge to the *Altertumswissenschaft* of Theodor Mommsen that dominated the second half of the century. From Boeckh, Burckhardt received the full training in all the aspects of ancient life. Important as this was, one may wonder whether Burckhardt was not even more impressed by Boeckh's vision of the totality of Greek life and civilization. Burckhardt's own history of Greek civilization was the belated fulfillment of Boeckh's project and one of the main themes of Burckhardt's treatment had already been sounded by Boeckh when he stated that the Greeks had probably been a much unhappier people than their art and poetry might indicate.

Still the profoundest influence that Burckhardt experienced in Berlin was the personality and teaching of Leopold Ranke. Burckhardt then and later made many sharply critical remarks about Ranke as a person and a historian. But Ranke taught him not only the new historical methods, particularly in the medieval field, but brought the young Burckhardt face to face with the fundamental problems of universal history. Burckhardt adopted much of the Rankean position but rejected many of Ranke's ideas as he grew to full maturity. Still, in the brief curriculum of his own life that Burckhardt wrote according to Basel custom to be read at his own funeral, he spoke of Ranke as the "great master." Let me mention on the side that Ranke followed Burckhardt's writings with interest and understanding and was quite active in trying to bring him to a German university.

The years 1839–43 which Burckhardt spent in Germany show the young Swiss deeply in love with that country. It was here that he finally decided to devote his life to history without any wavering. But this was only a part of his gratitude. He could say: "I am obliged to Germany for *everything*. My best teachers were Germans, at the motherly bosom of German culture and science I was nurtured . . ." and would exclaim: "and this people, this magnificent German youth and this country, God's garden! Am I worthy to tread this soil soaked in the blood of martyrs?" "Where would be all our freedom if Germany had not wrecked Napoleon?" Jacob Burckhardt in these years was not only an absolute admirer of German academic scholarship but also a sympathizer with the national and liberal aspirations of the German *Vormärz*. Yet the agreement with the national and constitutional movement, as he found it in Bettina von Arnim, Jacob Grimm, and even more among the friends of his own generation, like Gottfried Kinkel, weakened at the end of his German years. A visit to Paris filled him with horror about the actual consequences of modern constitutionalism. After his return to Basel the radical trends awakened grave forebodings. Burckhardt gave at the Basel University historical lectures but became a political editor of a conservative Basel newspaper in order to make a living. He quickly discovered that he had not reached the personal maturity nor acquired the knowledge to teach and write history as it should be in his opinion. In 1846 he left for Italy and in subsequent years, while the revolution of 1848–49 set the Continent in flames only to be superseded by the military Caesarism of Louis Bonaparte and violent reaction elsewhere, developed in seclusion the outlines of his own thought.

Though Italy was from now on God's garden and though

there was in Burckhardt's study and enjoyment of the historic monuments a strong epicurean note, it was at the same time a self-chosen departure from the world of his own age. It seems that at about this time he finally gave up all ideas of marriage as of active politics. He separated himself entirely from the liberalism that was the religion of most of his coevals. Burckhardt also turned away from the romantic admiration of Gothic art to a new classicism. In 1858, after having held for a few years a professorship in Zurich he became professor of history and later also of history of art in Basel. He rented two modest rooms over a bakery where he lived till 1897, giving all his outward efforts to the teaching of history in Basel. All offers of chairs in German universities, such as Heidelberg and finally in 1872 the succession to Ranke in Berlin, he turned down. (Both in Heidelberg and in Berlin, Treitschke accepted.)

Leaving aside some early articles and small studies, only four works of Burckhardt were published in his lifetime: *The Age of Constantine* in 1852 (second edition, 1880), the *Cicerone or Guide to the Enjoyment of Italian Works of Art* in 1855, the *Civilization of the Italian Renaissance* in 1860, the *Architecture of the Renaissance* in 1867. During the last thirty years of his life he did not publish at all and even turned over the revision of his original works to other editors. In his curriculum vitae, already quoted, he wrote that a small income had enabled him to avoid the slavery of the publishers, but no doubt his attitude also expressed his disdain of all the minutiae that the specializing historians of the second half of the century were producing in an ever-growing mass. Burckhardt meanwhile attended to his own tasks about which the world learned only after his death. In 1898 his *History of Greek Civilization* appeared, in 1905 his *Reflections on World History*. It would lead too far to enumerate all the works of Burckhardt, which have seen the light in the thirty years after his death. They are nowadays easily accessible in the critical edition of his works which was published in 1930–

33 by an eminent group of Swiss students of Burckhardt. They used the *Nachlass* and gave much new information from it, among it in the first place the *Historical Fragments* which augment his *Reflections on History* and are of fundamental importance for the understanding of Burckhardt's total conception of history. Simultaneously many volumes of Burckhardt letter exchanges have been published. Again, no time should be wasted here by listing these collections which throw light on many of the inner motives and aims of Burckhardt's historiography, which are the more important since Burckhardt in his works put his most intimate thoughts often in a veiled ironic form. A large consolidated edition of Burckhardt's letters is now in the process of publication in Switzerland.

The literature on Burckhardt is probably larger than that on any historian. Again I do not propose to discuss this literature except for mentioning that the present incumbent of Burckhardt's chair in Basel, Professor Werner Kaegi, is writing an extensive biography on the basis of all the Burckhardt papers. Of the extremely valuable and well-written work two volumes have appeared so far, bringing the story of Burckhardt's life to 1846.

II

Burckhardt, as has already been indicated, was a pupil of Leopold Ranke and never in his life departed from some of Ranke's basic conceptions of history. He shared from the outset Ranke's opposition to the philosophy of history of the Enlightenment or Hegelian type. A good many convictions were brought together in this attitude. First of all, it expressed the belief that all historical events and factors, though not necessarily unique in every respect, appear in an individual form and that consequently no general laws of historical development could be established. Thereby the possibility of projecting such laws into the future and predicting the outcome of events was meaningless. The idea of progress appeared particularly objectionable, the more so since it degraded all the past generations to a mere means for the achievement of the perfection and happiness of an ultimate golden age of the future. "Every generation is equally close to God," Ranke used to say. This necessitated, however, the exclusion of long periods of nascent or stagnant civilization as nonhistoric or prehistoric ages.

Vis-à-vis Hegel another common position can be discerned. To Hegel world history was the unfolding of the absolute spirit. The momentum of the movement of history and its true reality lay in the "self-activity" of the spirit and the outward appearances of history were only the masquerades or superstructures of the metamorphoses of the spirit that actually followed its own rules of logic. In Hegel's view it was, therefore, the philosopher who would be the true interpreter of history and could lead the way from logic to metaphysics. Ranke was utterly opposed to an interpretation of history that made the real historic institutions and events just the crustaceous shells of the only living kernel of history that was spirit. To Ranke the historical process was indivisible. The ideal did not only appear in the real, but the real often gave life to the ideal. In Ranke's words, the *"realgeistige"* is the essence of history and history cannot be understood by philosophical abstraction but only by the artistic visualization of the totality of history.

Before discussing the different treatments of history which are still possible under these general premises a third identity between Ranke and Burckhardt should be pointed out. The field of historical consciousness was the same. Universal history meant to both of them the history of Western civilization with some foreign influences here and there loosely related to them. Burckhardt went in certain respects beyond Ranke. He had for example more extensive knowledge of the Islam and had not studied Arabic in vain. But on the other hand the Islam was to Burckhardt not a dialectic element of Western history, as it was in some measure to Ranke, but rather a backdrop to European history, that allowed him by way of contrast to draw the contours of European phenomena more firmly. The scope of Burckhardt's vision of history covers substantially the same field as Ranke combined in his own universal history. It is the world of the Latin-Teutonic nations who succeeded, however, to absorb and preserve the legacy of the Greco-Roman civilization. The Middle Ages became in this view the crucial period of world history. They are the period in which the unity history, both in terms of peoples and of ages, was most fully realized. It must be emphasized that Burckhardt, the historian of the Renaissance, was a devoted student of the Middle Ages.

While Burckhardt was a loyal student of Ranke in many fundamental respects, he was early disquieted by certain results of Ranke's historiography. Hegel had taught that "what is, is reasonable" and that the great decisions of world history as expressing the wandering of the spirit through the phenomenal world must be considered with awe. Not chance ruled history, but absolute logical necessity, even the struggle of power found a complete metaphysical justification in the pantheistic view that world history was the autobiography of God in secular time. One can call Hegel's philosophy of history perhaps non-Christian, but there is no question that Hegel aimed at a restatement of a total explanation of the universe as the Christian religion of his youth had afforded. It was a secularized theology.

Ranke's position was different. He refused, as has been already said, to reduce world history to a spiritual process following logical laws. World history was to Ranke the miraculous tale of the human race, composed of human beings, pure and impure, strong and weak. Ranke remained a faithful Christian insofar as he never questioned that man had a destiny apart from and beyond secular history. Some have even pointed to links between Ranke and the old Augustinian construction of universal history as the great struggle between the two *civitates,* the kingdom of God and the kingdom of his earth. And, no doubt, the church or the churches had in Ranke's works still a somewhat independent role. But although Ranke opposed Hegel's pantheism, his own panentheism was probably not as far removed from Hegel as he himself and almost all of his followers in the last century have thought.

Ranke believed that world history, though not the history of God himself, was willed by God. It carried His imprints everywhere, and here and there His steps could be adumbrated by the historian. The story was not the full revelation of God's innermost being, but it was permeated with the divine essence. The first sentence of Ranke that Burckhardt heard was the opening phrase of Ranke's lecture course on German history in 1840: "Nations are the thoughts of God." History in Ranke's view was unthinkable if it was not planned by God. In all its unending variety it constituted innumerable reflections of His eternal reality. Ranke did not accept a teleology of history, like Hegel's progress of the spirit, nor did he identify as easily as Hegel the emancipation of the Absolute Spirit going from one to the next stage of world history with the decisions of power politics. But in actual fact Ranke did not remain too far behind Hegel in assuming that the real expressed the reasonable. States stood for principles and ideas. On the whole Ranke was convinced that the higher moral principles had been victorious in history and he even admitted that there had been through world history an accumulation of moral energies.

Ranke's views of history, though less exclusive than those of Hegel, were a secularized religion. Hegel's philosophy of history with its deification of the state and of power was perhaps more reckless than Ranke's historiography with its mild harmonizing of the grim realities of human history and the divine plan. But one could argue the case, for a moment at least, the other way around. It could be said that Hegel wrote his ideas into the sky, that somehow they were bold analogies between the metaphysical and human world, whereas Ranke's ideas were engraved into the rock of reality. This is a dangerous and exaggerated statement, but it may be said at least that in the later century, when the influence of the specialized studies was far greater than of philosophy, the Rankean point of view proved more impressive than Hegel's philosophy.

It was at this point that Burckhardt's dissatisfaction originated. Hegel's and Ranke's conceptions of history had grown in the period of tremendous political upheaval when the storm of the French Revolution and its son, Napoleon, threatened not only the old political authorities but also the very existence of the traditional national cultures of Europe with complete extinction. Hegel's political and philosophical thought was chiefly molded in the period of struggle, while Ranke's harmonizing ideas were formed at the time when the efforts of Napoleon to destroy the individual nations had failed and when in general the ideas of the French Revolution had been stemmed. Ranke was the child of the halcyon days of the Restoration when the traditional European system of states and the individual national civilizations were revived and the principles of the Revolution were subordinated to the old historic forces. The confidence in the continuity of the great historic institutions of the West is the nourishing flame that warmed and colored Ranke's universal and objective vision of the past. In different though not absolutely different ways Hegel and Ranke felt that their own system of thought preserved and restated the basic form of Western thinking, in which metaphysics had mostly been accepted as an integral element of *Weltanschauung*.

Burckhardt belonged to a new generation, the generation that developed its attitudes around 1840. It is the time when Karl Marx, incidentally born in the same year as Burckhardt, reached the critical stage of his intellectual growth, and when the by five years older Søren Kierkegaard published his first writings. There was hardly ever a generation that broke so radically with its fathers. For Burckhardt it was decisive that he lost his religious faith. Under the influence of his theological teacher, de Wette, and the historical criticism of the Tübingen school from Ferdinand Christian Bauer to David Friedrich Strauss the belief that the Christian religion enabled men to gain an insight into a transcendental order appeared as fallacious.

Burckhardt did not reach the conclusion that Christian religion was a mere myth nor that it was a fraud played on the people to strengthen and perpetuate political or class domination, in Marxian terms an opiate for the people. He did not deny that the Christian religion was in many cases a force imposed on people and not the spontaneous expression of their own inner life. But if the Christian religion had shown itself that potent, it was due to the power of self-denial and asceticism that its greatest representatives had displayed. The essence of Christianity Burckhardt saw in its otherworldliness, and though he did not overlook the political temptations to which the Roman Church succumbed, he thought that it gave on the whole a greater opportunity for the rise of otherworldly saints than Protestantism. Burckhardt thought eventually of the Reformation as a movement of those who wanted to lead an easier life. With regard to the present, he recoiled from all those people who called themselves Christians, though in spite of their professed religiosity they are not disposed to renounce the advantages and benefits of modern civilization. "The humble surrender of self and the parable of the right and left cheek are no longer popular."

There is much in Burckhardt's judgment on Christianity comparable to Kierkegaard's critique, but Burckhardt did not feel it his mission to restore Christian religion nor did he consider it historically possible to revive it in his own days. Said he: "that Christianity has outlived its great epochs is as evident to me as that two plus two make four." It is clear, however, that Burckhardt's loss of faith did not stem from any desire to get rid of discipline and authority and to turn to a pagan worship of secular and natural life. The loss of Christian religion is a bitter privation and by itself one of the main signs of the decadence of modern civilization, which, however, is threatened by other forces as well.

Early in his life, already before 1848, Burckhardt was gripped by fear about the consequences of modern nationalism, democracy, mass-education, and industrialism. He was no friend of democracy, but he did not believe that democracy would have an easy future on European soil. He foresaw that the popular mass movements of a democratic and socialist order would rather be exploited by strong men for power politics. He viewed with profound suspicion the usurpation of power by Louis Bonaparte and equally the violent methods of Bismarck. He was seriously concerned that the incapacity of modern society to integrate the new masses into the old culture would lead to the ultimate rule of demagogues. Burckhardt showed an uncanny foresight into modern totalitarianism and the rise of what he called the "terrible simplificateurs."

But we are not here concerned with Burckhardt as a political prophet but with the historian. In contrast to Ranke to whom universal history was a History Bible, the study of which could make you sense the plans and for that matter gracious plans of God, Burckhardt removed all metaphysical relations from the study of history. By giving them up, however, he was forced to go some steps further. If history was not the story of a meaningful progress of the human race, if on the contrary it seemed destined to enter on new and possibly worse crises, was it important to depict the full course of world history in the sequence of events and stages, what Ranke had called the *Mär der Weltgeschichte?* Burckhardt turned deliberately to another form of writing history. Whereas practically all of Ranke's works were vertical sections of history, all of Burckhardt's books were horizontal sections through history.

THE PHILOSOPHY OF
HISTORY OF KARL MARX*

BEFORE TURNING POSITIVELY to this afternoon's theme allow
me to define my subject more clearly in a negative fashion.
Limitations of time will make it necessary to leave out certain
matters. I have to confine myself to the major ideas in Marx's
philosophy of history and can present only the basic experiences behind the development of his thought. I must also
leave alone another problem, which is no doubt very interesting, namely the differences of opinion and philosophical theories between Marx and Engels. Friedrich Engels was in a
good many respects the more amiable of the two dioscuri, but
Marx was the more creative and original thinker. Consequently, my remarks will focus exclusively upon the philosophy of history of Karl Marx. Let me add on the other side that
I shall not deal with what happened to Marx's philosophy in
subsequent schools of socialism or communism. I am not concerned here with the impact of Marxian ideas on history.
Many present-day treatments of Marx, including one of the
recommended books of this course, Carew Hunt, *The Theory
and Practice of Communism*, project too many things from
modern communism or sovietism into the original Marx. An
Oxford scholar, John Plamenatz, is going to publish a book
called *German Marxism and Russian Communism* (London,

* Yale lecture, 1954.

1954), studying "the philosophical and economic system of Marx and what the Russians have made of it." There can be no question that this is a big question worth studying, but I cannot hope to discuss this problem today.

Marx's system of thought stemmed from German, French, and English sources. It cannot be explained only by considering his German background. But it is true that his German upbringing determined the growth of his *philosophical* ideas more fundamentally than that of his ultimate political and economic ideas. The German atmosphere in the formative years of Marx was profoundly steeped in philosophical and metaphysical speculation. In the fifty years between the appearance of Kant's *Critiques* and the death of Hegel the Germans had made their major intellectual effort in the field of philosophical speculation. From 1818 to 1831 Hegel dominated the scene from his chair in Berlin. Possibly the dominance of Hegelianism was even greater in the immediate years after the death of the imperious thinker, including the year 1836 when the young Marx came as a student to Berlin. Hegel and Hegelianism was undoubtedly the strongest philosophical influence that Marx experienced in his own life.

Hegel had given history a central place in philosophy. Prior to Hegel philosophers had been chiefly concerned with nature and the evolution of natural-scientific thought. With the exception of the lonely Italian Vico, history was not regarded a source of philosophical truth. Hegel placed history uppermost in philosophy. Through the study of history man's existence and man's destiny could be fully understood. To this extent at least Karl Marx always remained a pupil of Hegel. History in contrast to nature is the world of man, and from history, therefore, man must get a knowledge about human capacities and his own ultimate faith.

In Hegel's philosophy universal history was conceived of as the process of unfolding of the absolute spirit or absolute reason (*Logos*) or of God passing through the finite world. Since this absolute spirit was thus defined as rational the migration or peregrination of the absolute spirit through the finite or temporal world would have to follow in Hegel's eyes the laws of reason or, in other words, the principles of philosophical logic. "Everything that is, is rational" is the fundamental proposition of Hegel's philosophy. More explicitly stated this means: "Everything that is necessary in the progress of the spirit from one stage to the next one is rational." From this Hegel deduces the applicability of the law of logical dialectics, the sequence of thesis—antithesis—synthesis or affirmation—negation—negation of negation or reaffirmation, to history.

If we inquire into the personal motives and the ultimate intent of Hegel's philosophizing the intensity of his interest in politics is everywhere apparent. But his contemplative concern was even greater. At bottom it was a theological intention of restating the Christian faith in philosophical terms which would defeat the critique of historical Christianity that the Enlightenment had raised. In Hegel's fundamental proposition about the absolute spirit and its incarnation in secular history already this motive is clearly transparent. But Hegel's religion became a rationalistic pantheism which enabled him in his mind to organize the many centuries and the vast variety of contradictory phenomena of history, and feel himself at the same time under the light of an absolute idea. Salvation is achieved through the contemplation of the totality of the historical world. In this respect Hegel was a pure philosopher and this is further illustrated by his insistence upon the philosopher's incapacity for predicting the concrete character of the future. Philosophy of history was only able to create an ordered understanding of the past and not of the future. In his view, of course, future history would still follow the laws of dialectic, but what actual shape future ages would assume was beyond the ken of philosophical speculation. Hegel went as far as to admit that the world had already grown old and that the wanderings of the absolute spirit were approaching their end. Man's capacity of understanding instead of merely describing history, or in other words the very appearance of his own philosophy, seemed to him a proof that the absolute spirit was about to return to itself and rest in its ultimate abode.

Yet the Hegelian system grew out of the great revolutionary events which he witnessed in his youth and early manhood. The complete helplessness of Germany vis-à-vis the French Revolution and the subsequent expansion of France over Europe through Napoleon made Hegel accept the role and value of political power. The liberation of Germany in the wars of 1813–15 convinced him of the significant historical mission of Prussia. Hegel was no blind reactionary; he accepted many of the results of the French Revolution. Still he became a strongly conservative political philosopher and this was due to a large extent to his assumption that the function of philosophy was the interpretation of the past rather than the prediction of the future. Hegel's conservatism is usually stressed as the outstanding trait of his philosophical system. But in his philosophical contemplation there were also the seeds of activist thought and of radical and even revolutionary politics.

After Hegel's death in 1830, one group of his students, the so-called "young-Hegelians" or "left-Hegelians," began to emphasize just these activist elements in Hegel's philosophy. If one looked at world history in Hegel's fashion one saw one concrete form of historic life and civilization after the other grow up and soon thereafter perish. The underlying sentiment of Hegel's philosophy of history is perhaps best expressed in the remark of the satanic Mephistopheles in Goethe's *Faust: "Alles was entsteht, ist wert dass es zu Grunde geht"* (Everything that comes to life deserves to perish as well). This pessimistic and melancholy aspect of Hegel's philosophy of history was a strong element in Hegel's thought. And why should there be an end to this death and transformation in the present? Was the process of historical life not bound to go on to ever new forms and for that matter even to antithetical forms? If this was true, was the function

of philosophy the contemplative organization of the past or
the activist prediction of the future?

Perhaps even more serious in a critique of Hegel's thought
was his facile synthesis of religion and philosophy, although
the creation of a harmony between faith and reason was one
of the major objectives of his philosophizing. The entrance of
the Absolute Spirit into the finite world—I hinted at this before—must be considered a philosophical or secular transformation of the Christian view of history. But Hegel's pantheism
emphasized the rational character rather than the moral sin-
fulness of the world. In his monistic interpretation the Christian dualism of the struggle between light and darkness was
blotted out.

Moreover, in Hegel's philosophy the absoluteness of Christian religion itself became questionable. To Hegel world history was largely the peregrination of the Absolute Spirit mas-
querading in one costume only to throw it away for ever-new
masks. Inevitably this would apply to historical religion, including Christian religion, equally well. Every idea, may it be
a political or legal system or a religion, appeared to be only a
temporary manifestation of the Absolute Spirit. Ultimate truth
was to be found only in the totality of *all* historical forms and
expressions.

Once one followed this line of argument to its final conclusions all the religions, including Christianity, were only
metaphysical projections of the spirit of one or the other civilization or historic age. In other words, they were not the incarnation of a metaphysical idea. David Friedrich Strauss in
his epoch-making *Life of Jesus,* published in 1835, was the
first author to explain the life stories of Jesus, as contained in
the New Testament, as human myths. In 1841 Ludwig Feuerbach in his *Essence of Christianity* declared Christian religion
a mere fiction of man who created himself a God according
to his own image. With the assertion that religion and, for
that matter, all ideas were man-made, the metaphysical foundation of the Hegelian system became untenable. The concep-

tion of the Absolute Spirit as the origin, motivating cause, and end of history appeared as a philosopher's fairy tale. Hegel's general proposition, that everything that is, is rational, was not necessarily denied by this criticism. But the rationality of history could no longer be constituted as the operation of a transcendental spirit but had to be considered as the product of secular history.

II

This was exactly the position that the young Karl Marx reached under the influence of the young-Hegelian school, of men like Arnold Ruge, Bruno Bauer, Ludwig Feuerbach, all of whom, incidentally, he surpassed not only as an activist revolutionary, but also as a philosophical and historical thinker. The result of his Hegelian education was the historical materialism. Marx's famous statement, that with Hegel philosophy stood on its head and that he, Marx, had set Hegel "right way up," declared his opposition to Hegel's metaphysics. It implied that history was not the expression or realization of an absolute idea that exists prior to and beyond finite reality and consequently that what Hegel called the forms of the objective spirit, i.e., the appearances of the Absolute Spirit in the objective forms of civilization such as religions, states, etc., are also not manifestations of a transcendental idea but creations of human history itself.

Actually this cannot be called in any strict sense "materialism." In modern philosophical language, Marx's thought would be called either "realism" or—probably better—"evolutionist naturalism." It is not matter that produces historical events. Nor is it matter that produces thought, let us say, by chemical changes in the brain cells or veins or what not. Karl Marx was only a radical and absolute antimetaphysicist, but not a true materialist. What he wanted to express when he called his philosophy of history "materialism" was his disbelief in a transcendental source or transcendental goal of history. History was to Marx essentially the growing control of man over nature.

In spite of this radical shift from Hegel's idealistic position Marx retained the dialectic as the fundamental law of historical development. Philosophically this can hardly be sustained. Dialectic, which means the application of the laws of logic to history, could perhaps be defended as long as history was conceived as a development of *logos*—spirit, mind, reason, or whatever translation you want to use. But if history was understood as a secular process why should then the laws of logic apply?

Moreover, in Hegel's philosophy history had a clear beginning and end, as well as a definite dynamic principle. It was the self-exploration of the spirit beginning with its self-alienation and rising through the torments of history to its ultimate self-realization. However, if history was, as it was to Marx, a finite and nontranscendental series of events, where could one find a principle of historical progress? Yet, Karl Marx retained not only dialectics but also Hegel's definition of progress as "progress in the consciousness of freedom." In Hegel's contemplative philosophy progress lay in the growing capacity of man to understand his historical station in the progress of the Absolute Spirit. To Marx it was progress toward the full and literal realization of freedom on earth. Actively bent on this aim, Marx found fault with Hegel and all his philosophical predecessors. As he put it: "All philosophies have sought to explain the world; our part is to change it."

This activist element of Marxian thought cannot be traced back to Hegel and maybe not at all to the German idealistic philosophy, although there are possibly some such trends in Kant. Karl Marx was largely formed by a novel historical experience, for whose interpretation he relied heavily on the contemporary Western European thought. The basic practical experience in Marx's life was the impression of what is usually called the Industrial Revolution. Among Germans of his generation probably only a man from the Rhineland could have fully faced up to the phenomenon, since Germany at large was still an unindustrialized country except for the Rhineland, which partook in some measure in the earlier beginnings of the industrial revolution of Western Europe. This is the chief reason that made Karl Marx an ardent student of Western European thinking. What aroused his moral ire was the devastating influence of the growth of natural science and technology on the life of man. The observation of the dehumanizing impact of capitalistic machine production caused not only wrath in him but made him marshal all his personal strength to fight the evil. Science and technological invention ought to establish man's complete mastery of nature and should, therefore, be the means of the realization of human dignity and freedom. Here Marx stood in the tradition of eighteenth-century Western Enlightenment and the law-of-nature school which Hegel had fought to the utmost.

Under the impression of the early Industrial Revolution Marx judged that the progress of society depended on a change in the conditions of economic production, which in the capitalistic system perverted the potentialities of man. Marx's philosophy was consequently not only "historical" and "dialectical materialism," it was also "economic materialism." From economics Marx derived the law of historical dynamics and progress. Thus it was logical that once he had gained what seemed to him an adequate general theory of history he turned the major effort in the latter part of his life to economic studies.

But before we concentrate upon the discussion of the meaning of "economic" materialism let me emphasize again that at least with regard to the goal of history Marx's philosophy was not materialism. Marx himself could originally speak about his system of thought as the philosophy of true humanism or later as the genuine heir to English and French socialism and German idealism. No doubt, the aim of his philosophizing was to set man free for the pursuit of his personal happiness but even more for the untrammeled use of his highest intellectual faculties. Socialism is only the means through which this state of humanity is to be achieved. In this very unmaterialistic faith of Marx much of the appeal of his doctrines to the masses rests. It is, incidentally, one of the reasons why Marxism cannot be fought exclusively with mere materialistic weapons. A policy of raising standards of living by itself will not cope with the humanistic or even religious forces of Marxism.

With these reservations in mind let us turn our attention to economic materialism. The faith in the liberating power of socialism was to Marx not religion but science. In contrast to what he called the "utopian" socialism of the earlier period Marx maintained that his socialism was "scientific." Former schools of socialism had made chiefly an ethical argument. The goodness of man had been perverted by wrong and bad economic institutions. The purity of man must be restored by economic reform. In contrast Karl Marx contended that capitalism, no doubt, endangered human nature but that it could not be cured by moralistic appeals as such. Past and future of history, however, were bound by the immanent forces and laws of economic development which by themselves in spite of struggles and crises will bring on the ultimate realization of all the human potentialities. In other words, by the application of dialectic materialism history is given an ineluctable course from which it cannot be diverted. The future course of history, therefore, becomes scientifically predictable.

This construction of history was for the first time clearly presented in the *Communist Manifesto* and Karl Marx adhered to it with little change ever thereafter. From the original communist and classless but inarticulate society, in which all conflicts were still latent, class division develops originally as the result of the sexual slavery of women. This established the first situation in which social relationships of inequality, dominance, exploitation, and dependence became established. From there on classes stand up against each other in ever-new forms in a continuous struggle that reaches its absolute stage in capitalism, when essentially only two classes, the bourgeoisie and the proletariat, face each other. Finally an ultimate "catastrophe" will occur. The proletariat, exploited and driven back to exclusive reliance on its pure human resources, will rise and achieve the age of full humanity, a state of history in which man's faculties can grow and bloom freely. This is the state of classless society in which no further conflict and crisis should be expected.

A word may be said about this Marxian vision of history in its similarity and contrast to the romanticist version of history. The notion that the new capitalism as well as the bourgeoisie were forces of social disintegration was widespread among the conservative thinkers of Europe in the first half of the nineteenth century. But their ideal society was the social order of the Midddle Ages, in which a complete harmony between idea and reality had existed. Modern mechanistic and rationalistic thought had disrupted this ideal unity. There is as a rule a similar criticism of capitalism and the bourgeoisie in the conservative thinking of the period, but the romanticists look back to an ideal past which they wish to restore. For Marx history is the preparation of an ideal future. For this reason, however, every stage of history has significance within the necessary total process of history. One can hardly find more laudatory praise of capitalism than in the *Communist Manifesto* and other writings of Marx. In his view capitalism appeared in history originally as a liberating force, destroying feudalism and through the creation of science and technology making possible a new stage in man's control of nature. Capitalism is a necessary stage of history, necessary for the destruction of the preceding feudalism and for the expansion of human capacity. But Marx can credit the bourgeoisie with the liberation from feudalism only to call it in the same breath the class of arch-exploiters, since capitalism in turn is only a phase in the progress toward freedom. But Marx would not urge workers to destroy all the achievements of bourgeois civilization. Machines were wrecked by workers whose livelihood appeared endangered by their introduction. Marx taught that the temporary hardships caused by technology had to be willingly suffered in view of the benefits which it conferred.

Marx's economic theories in the strict sense have already been critically reviewed by Professor Fellner. You have heard about the theory of surplus value, capital accumulation, ultimate catastrophe. Here we are interested in the interaction between economic and social development, since it is one of the main elements of his philosophy of history. Marxian economic determinism believes that economic production follows laws which men are unable to change. The conditions of production determine the forms of society and social groupings with their peculiar attitudes and ideas. Marx could say occasionally that the hand mill created the civilization of feudalism, the steam mill of capitalism. Even within the system of Marxian thought this placed an overemphasis on technology. Still, the remarks aim not at the technical inventions as such, but at the forms of organization of society which is imposed by the conditions of production. Economic and social history are interwoven rather than identical.

This leads me to my last point, the place of ideas in history. It is widely assumed that Kark Marx was not interested in ideas or that he found them powerless, since they were only rationalizations of economic motives. This is altogether untrue. It is correct that Marx thought no pure ideas existed in history because all of them were tinged by economic and social conditions. For this reason he called them ideologies rather than ideas or superstructures reflecting the situation of a given historical society or class. Such a sociological interpretation applied chiefly to the theories of the political, economic, and social order, but was extended by Marx, though sometimes with hesitation, to all ideas. But while thought and ideas are sociologically conditioned, they are by no means unimportant. On the contrary, while ideology is not the power that propels the engine, it is the transmission belt that keeps it moving. Only through ideology the dynamic of history becomes articulate and thereby real. Moreover, ideology, though always related to the development of economic and social conditions, progresses with history to the final stage of a classless society. With the disappearances of the class struggle, "ideology" will disappear as well, to be superseded by ideas or full philosophical truth. Marx is a true heir of Hegel and the German idealism in his belief that the evolution of history would lead to the ultimate revelation of absolute reason. Ideology was a very important matter, indeed, in Marx's philosophy and also in his strategy of revolution. In history, ideology was always in danger of becoming what Marx called "wrong ideology." As a matter of fact, even the consciousness of the proletariat is as a rule a false ideology, because the proletariat in its humble state falls victim to what bourgeois and other interests may inject into its consciousness. But with capitalism approaching its ultimate crisis, the objective chance exists for breaking through to final truth. This seemed to Marx the true function of the scholar. With the knowledge of dialectic materialism he will purify the consciousness of the proletariat which through revolution will not only bring on the end of the class struggle but also the end of all ideology in favor of pure truth.

I have endeavored to present to you Marx's philosophy of history by describing its underlying logical structure. What his successors made of it is not my subject, although it should be said that he cannot be totally absolved from all the guilt for many of the subsequent misunderstandings and crude simplifications of his teachings. But we should not forget that Marx has given modern historical thinking many important concepts. It is not economic determinism that makes Marx a great figure. Actually, many champions of capitalism are more one-sided economic determinists or—if you want—materialists than Marx was. But nobody before him had seen social classes as acting units of history instead of a mere agglomeration of individuals, and nobody had ever shown the necessity of what we call today the sociology of knowledge which no doubt has sharpened our conscience of truthfulness. Still, Marx's economic determinism tied the classes much too easily to economic motives. The historian of the past or the present knows of more than the two classes of the Marxian system and of other than the economic causes of class formation. A critical student of history will reject also the simple sequence of dialectic materialism. Our present age is not only determined by present-day forces but by forms of past ages.

The reality of history, which includes the totality of human nature, is only partially grasped in the philosophy of Marx. Thus, we may well use some of his propositions as practical hypotheses of study but must deny their absolute truth. As a prophet Marx himself has become a dated figure of the past.

WILHELM DILTHEY AND THE
CRITIQUE OF HISTORICAL REASON

I

IT MAY be doubtful whether or not Ortega y Gasset is right in calling Wilhelm Dilthey "the greatest thinker of the second half of the nineteenth century," but there can be no question that his work has a lasting place in the history of the past seventy-five years and has had an influence on contemporary philosophy that is still growing.

Dilthey was born the son of a Calvinist minister in the Rhineland in 1833, a year after Goethe's death and the year of Johannes Brahms' birth. He intended to study theology when he went to Heidelberg and Berlin, but before long philosophy absorbed all his interest. In 1864 he became lecturer on philosophy in Berlin, in 1867 professor in Basel, where he met Jacob Burckhardt. But before Nietzsche arrived there Dilthey had already gone to Kiel. From 1871 to 1882 he was professor in Breslau, where he formed a close friendship with Count Yorck von Wartenburg, a Prussian landed nobleman who was a philosopher of high rank.[1] In 1882 Dilthey returned to Berlin to occupy Hegel's chair for the next twenty years. He died at the age of seventy-seven in 1911.

Dilthey was highly regarded by his colleagues. His vote carried weight in faculty deliberations, and even more in the Academy of Sciences. His lecture courses, however, did not attract wide attention until the very end of the century, when they had to be given in the largest lecture hall of the university. His sudden success was probably only one more reason for his voluntary retirement at an early age. The last ten quiet years of his life were devoted exclusively to the completion of his work, though he probably knew he would not complete it, and certainly that he could not do so in the manner in which it had been begun. In his early forties he confessed to his mother: "It is strange how completely I have lost every worldly ambition in the wish to accomplish my great studies. The great crisis in the sciences and in European civilization in which we are living occupies my mind so deeply and completely that the desire to be useful in it has destroyed every personal ambition."[2] There was in him a lofty disregard of outward recognition by the academic world of his own time, which is the more impressive as he climbed the academic ladder so easily and successfully.

At the time of his death Dilthey was known as a man who had produced some of the finest studies in the history of philosophy and literature, in which he had created a new method of writing the history of ideas. He also received recognition for his role in the resurrection of German idealism, and in making a clear distinction between the methodologies of the natural and cultural sciences. But in this latter respect he was overshadowed by Heinrich Rickert, who systematized the logos of the age of William II so much more clearly that he imposed his concepts even on its critics like Max Weber. Dilthey's studies in anthropology and psychology were also frequently consulted as noteworthy investigations. But only some of his closest students, who knew the full sweep of his philosophy, dared to call the deceased a philosopher of higher rank than Nietzsche.

Dilthey's students prepared his work for final publication. The First World War interrupted this edition, and his most significant writings, which have made it possible to judge the real intent of his philosophizing, became available only during the twenties. Particularly important was the publication of volume V of the *Collected Writings* in 1924, of volume VII in 1927, and volume VIII in 1931. Today there are in all twelve volumes of *Collected Writings,* with one additional volume still unpublished.[3] Outside this collection we have the first volume of his *Life of Schleiermacher,*[4] a masterly study of the growth of the classic philosophical movement in eighteenth-century Germany. There is also the book *Inner Experience and Poetry,* among all his writings the most widely known in Germany. It was later supplemented by a posthumous publication *On German Poetry and Music.*[5] We have also important biographical sources, above all the correspondence between Dilthey and Count Yorck,[6] together with a volume of letters and notes of the young Dilthey.[7]

These publications have produced a rich discussion of Dilthey's philosophy. The most important contributions to a systematic study of Dilthey were made by Georg Misch, in his extensive introduction to volume V of the *Collected Writings,* and in his discussion of Dilthey's relations with the phenomenological and existentialist schools, written after the publication of Martin Heidegger's *Sein und Zeit,* which was profoundly influenced by Dilthey.[8] Among other German studies, the most notable is that by Otto Friedrich Bollnow, which modestly claims to be only an "elementary introduction" to Dilthey's philosophy, but is a most valuable guide in its interpretation both on account of the well-chosen excerpts from Dilthey's writings and of the author's comments.[9]

But Dilthey's influence has spread into other countries. The close contact between French and German philosophy created French interest in Dilthey. Some of his major works have been translated into French, and studies of him have appeared.[10] Even more has been done, however, in Latin America, where apparently Ortega y Gasset awakened an early interest.[11] In 1943–45 all of Dilthey's *Collected Writings* appeared in Spanish translation.[12]

Dilthey is still little known in the English-speaking world. He has exercised a very strong influence on R. W. Collingwood, in spite of the rather unsympathetic and partly misleading treatment in his posthumous *Idea of History*.[13] The small book by H. A. Hodges was the first serious English attempt at an analysis of Dilthey's work.[14] American interest in Dilthey started in an accidental and personal fashion. William James met him at the house of Hermann Grimm, the art historian, when he came to Berlin in 1867. He was greatly attracted by Dilthey and curious to learn more about him. He was quite disappointed that Dilthey parted from him without inviting him to his house.[15] Actually Dilthey himself was a mere visitor in the German capital and was on his way to Basel. If, however, he still remembered the meeting with William James in later years he must have regretted its briefness. He did not praise many of his contemporaries as highly as he did "the psychological genius of William James."[16] *The Varieties of Religious Experience* appeared to him the highest achievement in the psychological understanding of religion, the American contribution to the modern study of religion that began with Pascal, Lavater, Herder, Schleiermacher, and others.

It is impossible to say how deeply Dilthey studied the American pragmatism of his time and to what extent James or Peirce was aware of Dilthey. In retrospect Dilthey's "philosophy of life" and American pragmatism seem to have faced the identical problems of the age, and their answers offer many analogies. Both philosophies also show some anticipation of contemporary existentialism.[17] But American philosophy after James turned in other directions, and it was only twenty years ago that the first extensive critical report on Dilthey appeared.[18] Now, however, some of Dilthey's works are being prepared for publication in America.

II

The most decisive influence Dilthey received during his student years was exercised by the historians. When he came to

Berlin, Ranke was at the height of his career. He appeared, Dilthey said in later years, as "the personified capacity of the historical mind." But there was also the great historical tradition created by Niebuhr, Humboldt, Boeckh, the Grimm brothers, F. C. Baur, and others, and in addition the rich production of the next generation represented by Rudolf Haym, J. G. Droysen, Theodor Mommsen, Scherer, and the like. In these great achievements of historical research and writing Dilthey saw another expression of the prevailing trend of the modern age, which he called its "unsatiable desire for reality."[19] Its most powerful manifestation has been the growth of the natural sciences, which had been chiefly responsible for the collapse of the great metaphysical systems. This result Dilthey considered final, and he accepted Comte's construction of the three stages of human development, the religious, metaphysical, and scientific ages.[20]

Dilthey praised the Enlightenment for its confidence in the power of human reason and its secular interpretation of the world. He stated that it had been the dominant impulse of his own philosophical thinking "in the spirit of the great Enlightenment to cling to the world of experience as the *one* world of our knowledge."[21] This was said with reference to the theological metaphysics in which he had grown up; in later years he told his friend Count Yorck, who was a devout Lutheran, that "he did not even wish to gain salvation through a faith that could not stand up to thought."[22] In this attitude he did not differ from the positivists, or for that matter from the eighteenth-century philosophers, to whose creative achievements in philosophy, in the sciences, and in history as well he returned so often in his own great historical studies.

He attacked positivism, however, for its refusal to take all of reality into consideration. Quite apart from the metaphysical abstractions which linger on in it, positivism seemed to Dilthey "to mutilate historical reality in order to adapt it to the ideas of the natural sciences."[23] In particular, "it was based upon a truncated experience, which was from the outset perverted by an atomistic theoretical conception of psychic life." In contrast Dilthey claimed that it was the basic idea of his philosophy "that never before had philosophy been grounded on whole, full, unmutilated experience, and consequently never before on whole and full reality."[24] Positivism and empiricism show their failure most clearly in the cultural sciences (*Geisteswissenschaften*), which include not only history but also the study of language, law, economics, etc.[25] Dilthey does not deny that man is part of nature, and that, for example, physiology is one of the natural sciences. But as he puts it:

> Mankind, if apprehended only by perception and perceptual knowledge, would be for us a physical fact, and as such would be accessible only to the natural sciences. Man becomes an object for the cultural sciences only in so far as human situations are consciously lived, in so far as they find expression in living utterances, and in so far as these expressions are understood. . . . A study belongs to the human studies only if its object becomes accessible to us through the attitude which is founded on the relation between life, expression, and understanding.[26]

Before we trace, more slowly, the philosophical steps taken by Dilthey in these few statements, let us first inquire into his relation to Kant. He actually went back beyond Hegel and Fichte and their revival of metaphysics to the Kant of the *Critique of Pure Reason,* and in this respect he can be called one of the fathers of Neo-Kantianism. All knowledge is knowledge of experience, and the facts of human consciousness are the only secure foundation of philosophy. Dilthey calls this the "epistemological standpoint." He also follows Kant in the formulation of his own fundamental question: how are the sciences of the human mind—or humanities, or moral, or cultural, or historical sciences—possible?—exactly as Kant had asked how scientific knowledge is possible. The task of philosophy is not to create this knowledge, but to furnish its epistemological basis.

But Dilthey went beyond Kant in insisting that philosophy could not be exclusively concerned with natural science, but would have to explore the foundations of historical knowledge as well. In this sense he termed his own philosophy an attempt at the writing of a "Critique of Historical Reason." By defining his objectives in such a manner Dilthey wished to express his heritage from Kant, or rather his return to Kant. But at the same time there remained a sharp difference from Kant. Dilthey aimed at more than the mere addition of a new field to Kantian inquiry. In the preface to the *Introduction to the Cultural Sciences* he said:

> If I found myself often in agreement with the epistemological school of Locke, Hume, and Kant, recognizing with them in the facts of consciousness the whole foundation of philosophy, I was, on the other hand, compelled to conceive the interconnection of these facts in a different way. Neglecting the few, scientifically undeveloped attempts like those of Herder and Wilhelm von Humboldt, epistemology, whether empiricist or Kantian, explains experience and knowledge merely as belonging to the realm of thought. In the veins of the knowing subject that Locke, Hume, and Kant constructed runs no real blood, only the diluted lymph of reason in the sense of a mere intellectual activity. But I was led, by my historical and psychological study of the whole man, to make this whole man in the diversity of his powers, this willing, feeling, thinking being, the foundation for explaining knowledge and its concepts, such as those of the external world, time, substance, cause, however much it may seem that knowledge weaves these its concepts only from the material of perception, ideation, and thought.[27]

Two fundamental theses are contained in this and similar statements. The first concerns the conception of consciousness, the second, epistemology itself. Consciousness is to Dilthey not merely rational consciousness, but the sum total of feeling, volition, and thought. It is unrealistic to suppose that non-intellectual human activities will not interfere with man's thinking. Consciousness is given and can be experienced only as the totality of all the motives of the human mind. Intellectual consciousness cannot be isolated. What is given to us in our consciousness is the totality of our being, which Dilthey calls life, mind, spirit, or soul.

Dilthey rejects Kant's concept of a "pure" or "transcendental consciousness" and Hegel's "objective spirit" as metaphysical abstractions. He maintained that "thinking cannot go back beyond life," to which he added:

> Kant took time and thereby life itself to be merely phenomena. To consider life as mere appearance is a *contradictio in adjecto:* for in the lived life, in the growing out of the past, and in the tending of the self toward a future, lie the realities which constitute the dynamic unity (*Wirkungszusammenhang*) and the value of our life. If there were something timeless behind life, that runs through a past, present, and future, it would be an antecedent of life. Therefore, it would be the condition of the total structure of life. This antecedent would be just what we do not experience and, consequently, a realm of shadows.[28]

Dilthey's philosophy of life takes as its starting point life itself as it comes to consciousness in the individual as the act of living experience (*Erlebnis*). In this original act of living experience a full identity of subject and object exists. "In the act of living experience perception and the contents of my perception are one."[29] Dilthey expressed this once as "existence possessing itself," a formula that has played an important role in modern existentialism.[30] Living experience is an act that takes place in the individual and is determined by the totality of human faculties. The dominant chord in it may be intellectual, or religious, or aesthetic, or conative, and Dilthey is inclined to assign the higher significance to the three latter qualities of the human being, since thinking is actually the process by which reality is transformed into an object.

But this living experience is never a solipsistic experience. The self can never be alone, it exists always and inescapably among other human beings, and finds itself embedded in transpersonal relations with objects and other subjects. To be sure, there is a state of inner quietude, mere "dreams, play, diversion, contemplation, and light motility, like a deeper layer of life." But Dilthey adds:

> Living relations run in all directions. I react to men and objects, take a position toward them, fulfill their demands, and expect something from them. Some make me happy, expand my existence, augment my power—others exercise a pressure upon me and delimit me. . . . The friend is to him [man] a power which exalts his own existence, each family member has a definite place in his life, and everything that surrounds him will be understood by him as life and spirit which have objectified themselves in them. The shady tree, house, and garden gain in this objectification reality and significance. Thus, life creates its own world through the individual.[31]

In this description volition and desire are the agents which drive the individual beyond the indefinite state of quietude into a more definite state of individual activity. The individual, in the midst of the "relations of life" (*Lebensbezüge*) in which he finds himself, tries to cognize the world he experiences in a *Weltbild,* a word that has recently been introduced into the King's English as "world picture."[32] The "world picture" is the foundation of the experience of life (*Lebenserfahrung*), in which an evaluation of this experience takes place through feeling. Upon these values rest the ideals of life which determine the actions of man. It is not difficult to discover in these three layers the traditional definition of the faculties of the human mind as thinking, feeling, and willing. But it is important that Dilthey emphasizes the role of feeling in the totality of human consciousness. Indeed, most people never get beyond the *Lebensgefühl,* a feeling attitude toward life. This is not a definite but an oscillating position. "Continuously," Dilthey says, "the conception and evaluation of life and the world change, like shadows of clouds which pass over a landscape."[33]

It is the work of the religious, artistic, and philosophical genius to transform the feeling disposition into a conscious interpretation of reality, or, as Dilthey calls it, a *Weltanschauung,* a world view or outlook. It should be stressed that philosophy is only one among these three faculties, and the least fertile of *Weltanschauungen.* In his analysis of the artistic and philosophical movement of eighteenth-century Germany, Dilthey tends to credit the poets with the initial creation of the new outlook, which the philosophers from Kant to Hegel and Schelling translated into philosophical systems.[34] On the other hand, he was convinced, in spite of his emphasis on the historic place of Christian religion, that the full realization and preservation of monotheism was the result of Greek philosophy rather than Christianity.

It is the function of philosophy, by an analysis of the statements and premises of the *Weltanschauung,* to secure universally valid knowledge.[35] "Life is prior to knowledge."[36] But already in life itself there is inherent a propensity for higher consciousness. "Thinking can only increase the energy for raising the realities of life into consciousness."[37] But thinking not only has its roots in life, it also has a function with regard to life. "Life imperiously demands guidance by thought."[38] And more explicitly: "The progress of humanity in the modern age depends on its guidance by scientific knowledge. Therefore, the certainty of this knowledge must be defined and justified against the obscure feeling, the arbitrariness of subjectivity, and the skeptical mind, the ally of both."[39] Dilthey can say: "Philosophy is an action which lifts life, i.e., the subject in its vital relations, into consciousness and thinks it to its end."[40] Or finally: "Philosophy is only the highest energy of consciousness, the consciousness of every consciousness and the knowledge of all knowledge."[41]

III

But what constitutes scientific knowledge? With respect to the natural sciences Dilthey follows Kant. The experience that outward reality obeys the same laws we experience as the structural elements of our thinking, convinces us that our thinking is able to deal with this reality and to perceive its order. On this basis scientific research can proceed empirically within the framework of the general rules of reasoning without fear of mistaking speculations for facts. An outward criterion of the general validity of scientific results is to be found in their universal applicability, irrespective of their individual authors.

The cultural sciences are distinguished from the natural sciences both by their object and their subject of study. "One cannot have nature within oneself and by merely watching it learn what the world and life are and what they mean," he once wrote to his friend Count Yorck, and the latter said: "The whole psychophysical reality *is* not, but lives."[42] The only method by which a knowledge of man can be gained is through "understanding." We have already mentioned Dilthey's statement that living experience, expression, and understanding constitute the fundamental categories of the humanities. But we shall have to describe this process in greater detail.

"Understanding" of man, according to Dilthey, cannot be achieved by mere introspection or self-observation. Apart from the limitations of the life of any individual, even the greatest, introspection is conditioned by the questions I ask, and if I want to express them in words I find these words charged with a complex usage.[43] Living experience is an everflowing stream, and no lines and figures drawn on it would last.[44]

> *Inwendig lernt kein Mensch sein Innerstes*
> *Erkennen; denn er misst nach eignem Mass*
> *Sich bald zu klein und leider oft zu gross.*
> *Der Mensch erkennt sich nur im Menschen, nur*
> *Das Leben lehret jedem, was er sei.*[45]

The key to a more than merely subjective understanding of one's self as well as of other men lies in the "expressions of life." Dilthey distinguishes three major groups of "expressions of life." The first consists of statements of logical relations, which can be considered without reference to an underlying experience. The second group comprises actions, which we always try to understand as the result of the living experience of an individual or an individual group, though in Dilthey's words what they express is rather "undeliberate and nonintentional." The third group is made up of the expressions of living experience in the full sense. They stem from the urge "somehow to express the inner self, and somehow to place it before oneself or communicate it to others."[46] This is the ideal field of "understanding" and interpretation.

Dilthey does not disregard the second group of objectifications, and in particular he knows that there are actions which are produced by a highly conscious will. For instance, he sees the lasting contribution of the Romans to Western history in the new position they created for the will. Or, to take a different example, in his studies of the eighteenth century he pays attention not only to pietism, the philosophy of Leibniz, and the music of Bach and Handel, but also to the spirit underlying the codification of Prussian law under Frederick the Great. Still, as a rule Dilthey shies away from mere actions. "What springs from the life of the day is under the sign of its interests. Something terrifying lies in the fact that in the struggle of practical interests each expression can deceive, and the interpretation also changes according to our position." In contrast, a great work of art stands before you "truthful in itself, fixed, visible, lasting, and therefore an artistic and reliable understanding of it becomes possible."[47] The truthfulness of such a work is not to be judged in terms of right or wrong, but of its genuineness, which is determined by its capacity for achieving the full identity between expression and living experience. This applies not only to the works of the artistic genius, but likewise to those of the religious and philosophical.

Understanding becomes possible, since each individual knows from his own experience the process by which life tends to objectify itself in expressions. Man is driven farther and farther in the understanding of the human world by the discovery that a first primitive understanding proves an inadequate guide to the mastery of his practical problems. Life is action, and thinking that arises from life aims at a higher energy of action. But on all levels understanding remains a mere reliving of the living experience of oneself or others. The limits of the expansion of our understanding are set by this fact. We can relive only what is at least potentially given to us, or, as Dilthey would have said, what is contained in that dynamic unity of life (*Wirkungszusammenhang*) of which our individual life is a part.

"Life takes possession of life"[48]—in this formula Dilthey once expressed the difference between the cultural and the natural sciences in which phenomena are organized by means of abstract concepts. In order to avoid misunderstanding at this point, we must keep in mind that Dilthey called "cultural sciences" all the disciplines of knowledge dealing with man or mankind, or in other words not only the humane arts but also the social sciences, "history, economics, jurisprudence, political science, the study of religion, literature, poetry, architecture, and music, of philosophical outlooks and systems."[49] All these branches of knowledge are nothing but a systematic knowledge gained by living experience and understanding.

It also follows from this that the student of the cultural sciences does not necessarily have an advantage over the practical man. A statesman, for example, may have a much greater insight into personalities or into the interconnectedness of the factors in a political situation, though as a rule he may not care to lift them into clear consciousness, except with a view to his immediate practical purposes. On the other hand, no scholar can amount to anything who has not had some living experience in the field he wishes to advance. A political historian without a living interest in political action, a literary critic without poetic sense, a student of religion without religious feeling, etc., cannot hope to produce significant knowledge in his discipline. The cultural sciences require "aliveness" (*Lebendigkeit*) by the very nature of their form of knowledge.

Another misunderstanding must be avoided. Dilthey never shared the theory of the cultural and natural sciences developed by the so-called "southwestern German school" of Neo-Kantianism.[50] Following a suggestion by Wilhelm Windelband,[51] Heinrich Rickert built up the theory that the cultural and natural sciences could be distinguished philosophically as idiographic and nomothetic studies.[52] Whereas the sciences of nature aim at the establishment of laws, the *Kulturwissenschaften* by descriptive and comparative methods study man as he acts under the influence of moral, aesthetic, and intellectual values. Heinrich Rickert's definition of the general as the object of natural science and the individual as that of the *Kulturwissenschaften* induced him, in contrast to Dilthey, to place some branches of knowledge like economics or psychology among the natural sciences.[53]

Dilthey refused to adopt Rickert's distinction. To him the cultural sciences are not confined to the individual, but include as their main problem the relation between the individual and the general.[54] Moreover, as he said as early as 1883,[55] the *Geisteswissenschaften* are characterized by the combination of the historical, abstract-theoretical, and practical direction of interpretation. And in his last years he wrote: ". . . the recently much-used term *Kulturwissenschaften* contains an unprovable, nay one-sided definition of the meaning and goal of history. This is much too friendly and generous an interpretation of human nature, in which the dark instincts of mutual suppression and destruction play a very considerable role."[56]

Dilthey uses a much broader conception of "reality" than most of his Neo-Kantian colleagues. He defines it as "life," or, as he calls it quite often, "history." His definition of man as a man among men applies not only to the present but to a continuum in time. Dilthey would even go beyond this statement. The individual himself is a historical being, and the relations of the life in which he finds himself are historical. Not only do the actual political and social conditions mold the life of which the individual is part, but its forms of consciousness and expression are also determined by history. Therefore, introspection can never answer the question of what is man; only history can.

Dilthey expressed this idea, which distinguished his own philosophy of life sharply from that of Nietzsche, in words which, incidentally, do not do justice to Nietzsche's attitude toward history,[57] but express Dilthey's ideas quite clearly.

Nietzsche stands as a warning of where the brooding of the individual mind leads, which tries to grasp the essence of life within its own self. He denounced history, perhaps in disgust at its unlimited critical detail, without which it is not truly a science. He believed that he had to disregard everything that this history and the community had done to him; he peeled it off like skins one after the other. The core, the problem of what constitutes man, he thought he could then seize in an ever-new anguish of brooding about himself, as once Rousseau tried to find the natural behind the historical man. And this brooding about one's inner self, this ever-renewed self-observation, what did it find? Exactly what characterizes the present historical state of our economic life and of our society: the "living dangerously," the reckless expansion of one's own power. History from Euripides to the Renaissance had engraved upon his soul only this superman: the great trends of his age talked of him. Without pity the theory of evolution seemed to prove the supremacy of the man who conquers life. Thus, he found him in himself, as he could also have found quite different basic traits and could have formed them into an ideal. And out of him he made his abstract scheme of man, his abstract empty ideal.[58]

This statement places the emphasis upon the insufficiency of introspection, but it is equally concerned with the significance of history for a critical understanding of man. "Life contains as the first categorical definition, fundamental to all others, being in time (*Zeitlichkeit*)."[59] Natural events also occur in time, but time in nature and history are entirely different. Dilthey compares time in nature to "a line consisting of equal parts, a system of relations, like succession, contemporaneity, duration."[60] Time is nothing but the outward form, in which natural occurrences take place. In contrast to the formal one-dimensional time of nature stands the "real" or "concrete time" which is a substantial aspect of life itself.

"Concrete time consists . . . in the unintermittent advance of the present, in which the present becomes continually the past and the future the present."[61] The present is only a cross section of the continuous stream of life, and as such without extension. The present, therefore, is beyond experience in the strict sense. It cannot be defined in spatial or one-dimensional terms, but only by its contents. "The present is the fulfillment of a moment of time with reality."[62] We have the present always and everywhere, "where we suffer, remember, or hope, in brief, where we live in the plenitude of our reality"; but we always have simultaneously the consciousness of its moving into the past, "a feeling that at times overwhelms us to the point of acutest grief."[63] Dilthey stresses again and again what he calls the "corruptibility" of life. This means to him both the transitory character of life, which is in the hands of death at any moment, and the fragility of the particular contents of life.[64] In these views Dilthey moves closer again to Kant's transcendental metaphysics as the philosophy of the "boundaries" of man. His ideas have found a modern expression in Martin Heidegger's existential "anxiety" (*Sorge*) and "fear," though in this connection Kierkegaard should not be forgotten.

But there is another side to life. In contrast to the finiteness of life we have the experience of life as a continuous structural unity, in spite of the fact that we can have an experience neither of our own birth nor of our death. In this respect one can say that the life of an individual can be understood more fully by posterity than by himself.[65] In life, however, Dilthey argues, "the present includes the presentation of the past in the memory, and that of the future in the imagination, which explores its possibilities, and in the activity which sets ends among these possibilities. Thus, the present is filled with pasts and pregnant with the future."[66] In the continuity of these experiences the individual becomes conscious of being a self, extending in time.[67] But together with this consciousness of his own individual structure he acquires the awareness of ever more comprehensive structures of the general life, like nation and civilization, or finally universal history. On all levels understanding aims at grasping "significance" or "meaning" (*Bedeutung*). For "meaning" is the peculiar form of relation which the parts have to the whole in life.[68] Meaning is already the peculiar and also the true principle of synthesis in memory, and it is equally the fundamental category of historical thinking.

Yet meaning is established not only by contemplation but by active decisions as well. The past appears to us an inevitable and determined process, but we think of the future as a "possibility" and as a realm of active freedom. We may be wise enough not to consider it a world of absolute freedom, as, indeed, our interpretation of the past co-determines our actions, but we still consider the future as the world which we can hope to mold according to the lesser or greater power of our decision. The decisions we make by action are the choices among the possibilities we see in our imagination, according to the ends we will. But the actual meaning of the past begins to change, if the reality of life or history is augmented, so that a complete definition of the meaning of history would become possible only when history had come to an end.[69] Historical knowledge, therefore, cannot be identical through the ages, not only because the historian, like all other students of man, including the philosopher, suffers from the limitations of his finite historical position, but also because of the changing nature of his subject of study.

Dilthey had originally believed that all the cultural sciences had a common foundation in psychology. All of them needed in their work a knowledge of human nature, and if they wanted to achieve objective results this knowledge could not be based on subjective intuition or amateurish construction. But when, in preparation for the second volume of his *Introduction to the Cultural Sciences,* Dilthey reviewed psychological science he was dissatisfied with the existing schools. They claimed to be able to explain psychological facts but had not produced valid answers except in the borderland between psychology and physiology. All the higher forms of mental life had proved to them a sealed book.

Dilthey believed that the false methodology of psychology could be blamed for the failure of psychological research. It had modeled itself on natural science by trying to "explain" psychological events in terms of hypothetical principles to be verified by subsequent observation. Formerly psychology had taken its hypotheses from metaphysics, recently mostly from natural science. But Dilthey argued that the psyche or life of the human mind was not like nature an outer world which could be studied by using hypotheses in order to unify the unrelated perceptions of individual facts. The experience of psychological events is immediate, and there is no need to go outside or behind consciousness[70] by the injection of hypothetical explanations. Psychological events carry within themselves a unifying pattern, a "structure" that does not call for an explanation by general laws and hypotheses but only for analysis and description.

Dilthey presented in 1894 the blueprint of a "descriptive and analytical psychology."[71] The new psychology rejected the whole approach of natural science to psychology as incapable of dealing with the great and significant creative actions of the human mind and particularly of penetrating into the world of history. Experimental and explanatory psychology can deal at best with certain aspects of the psychological attitudes of present-day men, but it has no way of experimenting with historical man, which means that it has to exclude most of the sources from which we must hope to gain a knowledge of man. In addition, if "scientific" psychology were to live up to its presuppositions it would have to reduce the vast psychological reality to the interaction of sensation and feeling. Such individual acts were considered the primary psychological facts out of which the psychological world could be built.

Dilthey realized that this "scientific" psychology was incapable of ever coming to grips with the true psychological reality. By confining itself to primitive sensations and feelings, like those of pleasure and pain, it excluded the contents of the human mind and became formalistic. In contrast, Dilthey demanded a "realistic" psychology or "psychology of content" (*Realpsychologie* or *Inhaltspsychologie*). A realistic and empirical analysis of psychological events will show the indissoluble interconnectedness of cognition, feeling, and will in all of them. The attempt to isolate a single function of the human mind is an arbitrary abstraction. Moreover, even to make the single individual the basic unit of psychological study is unrealistic. The individual is a member of society; by its civilization he is molded, while most of his actions and reactions are determined by social habits and values.

The main task of a descriptive psychology is the study of

the structures by which the various functions of the human mind are organized. The great documents of human self-introspection, like Augustine's, Pascal's, or Goethe's auto-biographical works, and in general the insights into human affairs amassed in literature, poetry, and historiography, will be important sources for such studies. This material should be critically analyzed and systematized to find the typical structural forms of the human mind, and to investigate the problems of individuation, and of the creative achievements of man.

Dilthey's "psychology of structure" or, as he often called it in later years, "anthropology," was a marked departure from the psychological schools of the two Mills, Spencer, Taine, Fechner, and Herbart, though there had already started a certain movement away from sensationalism. It found expression in Wundt and most strongly in William James. Dilthey praised again the latter's "amazingly realistic power and capacity of inner perception,"[72] but he complained about James's relapse into metaphysical hypotheses, in so far as James attempted a correlation between psychological and physiological events. Dilthey refused absolutely to accept a causal explanation for the higher processes of the human mind.

Dilthey's approach has had a great influence on the development of modern psychology. In contrast to the old atomistic psychologists he emphasized the interconnectedness of all the functions of the human mind and of its creative capacity. Dilthey also stressed the inseparable link between the psychology of the individual and social psychology. It was Karl Jaspers, then still a psychiatrist, who developed Dilthey's ideas further in his *Psychologie der Weltanschauungen*.[73] Jaspers called his work a study in "understanding psychology," which he conceived as a cultural science in contradistinction to "experimental psychology," which belonged to the natural sciences.[74] Eduard Spranger, a personal student of Dilthey, in his *Lebensformen*[75] offered a typology of man, distinguishing six fundamental types: the theoretical, economic, aesthetic, social, political, and religious man. Modern *Gestalt* psychology also has some roots in Dilthey's descriptive psychology, and MacDougall, Freud, and Jung are to a varying degree indebted to Dilthey.

While Dilthey's "psychological" ideas thus bore rich fruits, they did not in his own opinion fulfill his original hope that psychology could be established as the foundation of all the cultural sciences. His descriptive and analytical psychology was only a cautious systematization of the inner experiences of the present and past as presented by the cultural sciences themselves. His attempt to find a common foundation for all the cultural sciences soon shifted from psychology to logic and epistemology. In the last period of his life he endeavored to build up a theory of interpretation or "hermeneutics." The problem had been with him since his early years, and no one knew its history as well as he[76]; but now he turned to its full philosophical analysis.

All the cultural sciences aim at "understanding" (*Verstehen*), and they try to understand something internal through the analysis of its outward manifestations. Of this attempt Dilthey now said: "It is a common error to consider psychology as our knowledge of this inner side of the spiritual process of life."[77] He began to draw a sharp distinction between soul and mind. Soul is the inner life of the individual, whereas mind is an objective entity. The meaning of a work of art is not to be found in the psychological experiences of the creative artist, but in forms and relations which belong to a deeper layer of life. Similarly, a political system or a system of law is not the expression of individual souls but of an objective mind.

Dilthey presented these ideas at the very time when Edmund Husserl, the founder of modern phenomenology, was banishing psychology from philosophy.[78] But Dilthey was far from retreating into an unhistorical Platonism. He continued to believe that a knowledge of man could be gained only from history. But he began to consider the objectifications of life, like religion, art, science, politics, economics, law, etc., as philosophical organs for an objective comprehension of man, since they were, as he once said, manifestations of the "immanent transcendence of life."[79] Dilthey put forth these ideas rather tentatively while he was trying to prepare the final statement of his philosophical position which his death made impossible.

Closely connected with these studies of his last years were his efforts to redefine the task of philosophy itself. Like Hegel, Dilthey believed that philosophy could expect a solution of its questions only from history, but Dilthey could not accept Hegel's absolute spirit as the prime mover of the historical process. The historic systems of philosophy constitute the highpoints in man's own understanding of himself and of the world. They are not the reflections of the movement of the absolute spirit, but the demonstration of life's own capacity to rise to higher levels. Philosophy consequently is the highest expression of life, through which it advances to new stages. The unity of philosophy does not rest in its actual statements but in its power to realize the creative nature of life by the ability to raise experiences into consciousness and transform them into systematic ideas.[80]

Dilthey demanded a philosophical study of the historical forms of philosophy with a view to its general function in translating life experiences, as expressed in world pictures and world views, into philosophical systems. By such study we could hope to see the full breadth of human self-expression and advance to a greater human self-understanding. The systematic study of world views, *Weltanschauungslehre,* leads to a new speculation on philosophy itself which Dilthey termed "philosophy of philosophy."

The philosophical systems which have appeared in history are relative, and though they have a unity in their common origins in life, their substantive statements cannot be harmonized. There are three major and irreconcilable types of philosophy beyond which the conflicting schools of philosophy cannot be reduced. Dilthey names naturalism, the idealism of freedom, and objective idealism as primary types of philosophy. Democritus, Epicurus, Hume, and Comte are representatives of naturalism; Aristotle, Kant, Fichte, Bergson, and William James, of the idealism of freedom; the Stoics, Bruno, Spinoza, Leibniz, Shaftesbury, Goethe, Hegel, Schelling, and Schleiermacher, of objective idealism.[81]

These types are not always pure; they are rather the points around which all philosophical interpretations crystallize. But the irreducible character of these types of philosophy proves at the same time that "the conflict of world views remains insoluble."[82] Dilthey tried to overcome the difficulty by assuming that life itself is "many-sided,"[83] and that each philosophy "expresses within the limits of our thinking one side of the universe. Each is true in this respect. Each is, however, one-sided. We are denied seeing these sides in unity. The pure light of truth we can see only in broken rays."[84]

The ideas of his last years have come to us only in fragmentary drafts for his projected last work, the second volume of his *Introduction to the Cultural Sciences*. He was not able to present them in systematic manner. But the general trend of his thought is clear and it has had a significant influence upon contemporary philosophy.

IV

Dilthey was a philosopher, but the significance he attached to history as an organ of philosophy made him a historian as well. He was both a great and original historical thinker and a master of historical presentation. His philosophy did not clash with modern historiography. Dilthey rejected completely philosophies of history of the Voltairean, Comtean, or Hegelian type and accepted the general methods of the nineteenth-century historians as the only possible approach to an understanding of history. His own research had made him fully familiar with all the problems of the historical profession. He struggled with the critical edition of Schleiermacher's letters, with the organization of a final Kant edition, and with the interpretation of the unpublished papers of the young Hegel. In brief, he knew the customary worries, thought processes, and methods of the practicing historian from his own research.

But, on the other hand, in contrast to the professional historians of his age who tended to lose sight of the philosophical implications of their methods and findings by embracing a vulgar empiricism modeled after the natural sciences, Dilthey was aware of the philosophical character of historical studies. This enabled him to criticize constructively the work of the nineteenth-century historians and to add to it by his own historical writings.

Dilthey maintained a profound admiration for Ranke all through his life. Ranke had displayed a unique will and power in achieving historical objectivity and had been the first "to express fully that the foundation of all historical knowledge and *one* of its highest aims is the presentation of its singular form of connectedness."[85] But this major interest led Ranke to an overwhelmingly aesthetic and "ocular" presentation, and political history offered him the greatest opportunity for composing history in a dramatic and panoramic manner. Though Dilthey probably did not quite agree with his friend's mocking remarks, Count Yorck's statements about the "magic lantern" or "rug-weaving" technique of Ranke[86] may serve as an indication of the direction of Dilthey's criticism of the Rankean history.

In Ranke, Carlyle, and Tocqueville, Dilthey saw the three greatest nineteenth-century historians, in whom the rise of modern historical consciousness had found its most forceful expression. A true Fichtean, Carlyle looked for the historical man and hero. He approached history not by "optical" means, but as a problem of inner life or of the relation of faith and action. Alexis de Tocqueville Dilthey calls "the greatest analytical mind in politics since Aristotle and Machiavelli."[87] As most clearly demonstrated in his classic study of American democracy, Tocqueville tried to isolate the individual elements important for the internal structure of nations and to show the interaction of the various functions in a modern body politic.

Still, Dilthey felt that historical interpretation was not exhausted by Ranke's generation nor by the work of his own contemporaries. His personal concern lay originally in the history of philosophy and religion. He studied the works of the so-called Tübingen school, whose father was the church historian F. C. Baur and whose chief historian of philosophy was the latter's disciple E. Zeller. The history of ideas, religious or philosophical, was to them a self-contained process of intellectual progress or, in Hegelian terms, the unfolding of the absolute idea in the world. The views of the Tübingen school continued to affect very profoundly the conceptions of Christian history expounded by the Ritschlian school in the latter part of the century, of which Adolf Harnack was the most brilliant representative,[88] and in the Neo-Kantian history of philosophy of Wilhelm Windelband, though increasingly the influence of Schleiermacher and his emphasis upon the creative role of the individual made its weight felt.

Dilthey did not believe that this type of history of ideas was capable of furnishing an adequate interpretation of intellectual and religious history. Philosophical and religious ideas spring from the totality of man's living experience. They have to be understood in terms of their origins in this living experience. The study of the living experience, world picture (*Weltbild*), and general world view (*Weltanschauung*) of every age is a prerequisite for a true historical understanding of religion and philosophy. The conception of a separate "history of ideas" is a mere abstraction. *Ideengeschichte* has to be replaced by *Geistesgeschichte*, i.e., a study of the efforts of life to achieve consciousness of itself. Religion and phi-

losophy are only "expressions of life," though expressions of
the highest potential of life. Dilthey added art to religion
and philosophy as an expression of this creative vitality.
We have already seen why this seemed so important to him,
and it is not surprising that a major part of his own historical
studies, which altogether form half of all his writings, was
devoted to defining the place of poetry, literature, and music
in the process of history.[89] They give, however, only a seg-
ment of his view of history.

We find the ripest fruits of Dilthey's historical interest in
such studies as "The Conception and Analysis of Man in
the 15th and 16th Centuries."[90] The title of this article, which
is a classic in modern historiography, is indicative of Dilthey's
historical intention to present the totality of life and analyze
its expressions in terms of a critical philosophy of life. The
term *Geistesgeschichte*, which literally means history of the
human mind, may lead to the belief that Dilthey conceived
of history as a mere reflection of the spiritual life of man.
It should be clear after our discussion of Dilthey's conception
of life and mind that such an interpretation would be untenable. In his analysis of historical life Dilthey always remained aware of economic, social, and political institutions
and events.

In this respect Dilthey's theory of history opened up certain
possibilities for the study of the social conditions of consciousness, and both the "sociology of culture" (Alfred
Weber) and the "sociology of knowledge" (Karl Mannheim)
found in Dilthey suggestive ideas.[91] Still, Dilthey was far from
identifying the material conditions of life with the "expressions of life." He never found it worth while to discuss
Karl Marx. What separated him from Marx was his belief
that "the meaning of history can only be looked for in the
significant interrelations of all the forces which are united
through the ages."[92]

One might suspect that Dilthey was in greater accord with
the history of culture (*Kulturgeschichte*), as represented in

his own time by many writers. But though Dilthey admitted
that history should not only deal, as in Ranke's work, with
events but that it should present the conditions and states of
civilization as well, he warned against disregarding the interrelations between the causal and chronological moments of
history. History is thus dissolved into the atomic elements,
which then have to be grouped under general categories.[93]
Dilthey speaks only with scorn of those histories which present civilizations under such chapter headings as court life,
home life, costumes, manners, etc.

But even Jacob Burckhardt's *Civilization of the Renaissance,* whose brilliant qualities Dilthey was quick to recognize in his review of 1862,[94] he praised only with strong
reservations. He found that Burckhardt, in spite of sharp
differences in historical methods, was still a descendant of
Ranke in his largely aesthetic approach to history. Ranke
had used individual events bound together by causal relations
as the firm framework of historical narrative. Burckhardt
aimed at the description of the general state of a historic
civilization as revealed in its intellectual and artistic achievements as well as in its social aspirations. Dilthey criticized
Burckhardt's concepts as not genuinely historical categories.
His description of the qualities of "Renaissance man" whom
Burckhardt conceived as the "the firstborn modern," could be
applied, and perhaps with even better right, to other periods
of history, for example, to the early period of the Roman
Empire. Dilthey also raised doubts about other central ideas
of Burckhardt, like individualism, as adequate descriptions
of Renaissance thinking. Burckhardt's terms, in Dilthey's opinion, were lacking in historical as well as philosophical concreteness, and were terms often used for artistic rather than
scientific purposes. A valid structural pattern could be found
only in the living experience of the historical generations
themselves. Thus his own "Conception and Analysis of Man
in the 15th and 16th Centuries" became, almost thirty years
later, his final answer to Burckhardt.

The cultural sciences—and they include (in addition to history) law, economics, political science, language, literature, art—are to Dilthey the means of experiencing the full potentialities of man, and the only way to expand the subjective self into a consciousness of the objective "expressions of life." History is more than a presentation of a phenomenal world, or a mere visualization of a dead past. It is the living experience of the student of history as well. Therefore history must also be a way of understanding the world.[95]

But history teaches the existence of a large variety of "expressions of life," determined by the passing conditions of historic time. In Dilthey's words, "historical consciousness demonstrates ever more clearly the relativity of every metaphysical or religious doctrine which has appeared in the course of time."[96] History appears as "a vast field of ruins of religious traditions, metaphysical positions, demonstrated systems, possibilities of all sorts."[97]

This may lead to despair, and in any event to mental suffering. For life points beyond itself, and though religious and metaphysical systems can only be considered historical expressions of life, the metaphysical and religious disposition is an essential quality of the human spirit. But over against the "anarchy of convictions" which frightens the modern historical mind stands the positive achievement. "Modern historical consciousness breaks the last chains which philosophy and natural science could not tear apart. Now man stands completely free."[98] It is important to look not only backward but forward as well. It is true that the objectivations of life are bound to pass and be followed by new ones, but these will be created by man. In spite of his own finiteness in time, man has creative capacity. New objectivations of life may wither in time, but they add a new meaning to life as a whole. For life itself grows, and it grows through man.

ERNST CASSIRER

WITH THE PASSING of Ernst Cassirer one of the great philosophical interpreters of human civilization has been taken from us. The last true scion of the classic tradition of German idealism has been laid to rest. While we are wondering whether the Germans will ever be able to produce a new moral and intellectual order by returning to the liberal humanism of their own past, which they renounced so violently in recent decades, this meeting is a demonstration of our confident faith in these ideas as a precious part of our own culture.

Soon after the classic school of German philosophy had been deprived of its great creative leaders with the deaths of Hegel and Schelling, German philosophy lost its dominant position to the new natural and historical sciences. Simultaneously German philosophy began to retreat from an active participation in the discussion of the fundamental political issues of the age. The programs of the political parties were little affected by the humane philosophy of the early part of the century.

In the last third of the century, however, a renascence of philosophical thought took place, which is usually called the rise of Neo-Kantianism. But though a great deal of the new philosophical discussion centered around a fresh study and appreciation of Kant, the new philosophical movement did not aim at the enthronement of the Königsberg philosopher as the patron saint of a new scholasticism but had much broader and deeper objectives. It sprang from the moral and intellectual dissatisfaction with the then fashionable ideas which seemed incapable of overcoming the growing materialism and naturalism. Many went even so far as to consider these philosophies the logical outcome of modern scientific research. In contrast, the new generation of German philosophers asserted that the progress of the individual natural and historical sciences stemmed very largely from the discoveries of classic philosophy and that research would lose its direction and meaning without a critical awareness of its basic methods. However, philosophy was not only to act as a guide to the various academic departments but was to gain fresh vigor from them.

Ernst Cassirer began his studies when the new philosophical movement had already gained influence in German universities. Lotze was probably the chief bridge-builder between the classic idealism and the neoidealism which then found its leaders in Dilthey and in the Neo-Kantian schools of Marburg and the Southwest, represented by Cohen and Natorp and by Windelband and Rickert. But it should not be forgotten that the sciences and arts took an active part in producing the new philosophy. German mathematics and physics from Helmholtz to Planck and Einstein were deeply conscious of their philosophical roots and not all the historians got lost in contemporary national politics. Harnack and his school of ecclesiastical history, the school of the history of religion from which Troeltsch made his way into philosophy, and Meinecke's work in the history of ideas are only a few examples of the manner in which historians helped to buttress the new philosophical movement.

Ernst Cassirer took his place among the best scholars of this group, and while he remained always grateful for being the member of a group of common spirit and purpose, he soon began to chart a course of his own in accordance with his personal gifts. In his early studies Cassirer concentrated on achieving a fuller understanding of the much-praised and little-known Leibniz, the real founder of the German philosophical tradition. Leibniz was the father of the theory of knowledge which, in contrast to almost the whole philosophy of the eighteenth century, Kant included, saw in the study of nature and of history two manifestations of the one human quest for knowledge. He did not consider the humanities a lower, or less mature, form of academic achievement. Both were branches of *Wissenschaft,* science, i.e., both were producing scientific truth though by different methods. Throughout his life Cassirer remained a student of Leibniz by keeping abreast both of the progress of the natural sciences and of the liberal arts.

However, Cassirer believed that his basic approach to philosophy was Kantian in origin. Kant had maintained that the way to a transcendental order could be gained only through an analysis of the forms and methods of human thought, and he had demonstrated the power of his new critical idealism in the philosophical study of the natural sciences, ethics, and finally aesthetics. The Neo-Kantians and particularly Cassirer went farther. Their epistemology included the methodology of history and moreover of all forms of creative civilization, finally encompassing even the expressions of pre-scientific human thought and imagination as revealed in language and mythology.

This is the key to the truly universal scope of Cassirer's studies. In addition to Leibniz and Kant, it was the spirit of Goethe which gave life to Cassirer's thought,

> *Wer nicht von 3000 Jahren*
> *Sich weiss Rechenschaft zu geben*
> *Bleibt im Grunde unerfahren*
> *Muss von Tag zu Tage leben.**

* Tr.: He who cannot account for 3000 years is basically inexperienced and therefore can only exist from day to day.

In Cassirer's personality and work Goethe's program of education became a living reality again. The totality of Western civilization was to be reconstructed and made a part of the consciousness of the modern individual and of present-day civilization. The study of the processes and creations of civilization would lift the individual to a position from which he could see farther than "from day to day" and could begin to grasp the ideal forms and categories of the human mind.

In this version of idealistic philosophy philosophical studies became in large sections identical with historical research. In general, Cassirer confined his historical interest to the history of human thinking and avoided the discussion of the social and political forces. However, he was not satisfied with the old-fashioned type of history of philosophy which dealt chiefly with the doctrines of the leading philosophers, and linked them together by a loose chain of abstract speculation. Thus, between a social and political interpretation of historical civilization on one side and a history of mere ideas on the other his history of human thought held its own place. His work ranged from the tedious editing of small texts and discoveries to his monumental edition of Kant. Beyond the editing it proceeded to the analytical and interpretative monographs and articles covering ancient science and the philosophy of practically all ages of Western civilization. Even those historians who care little about philosophy cannot bypass the new historical vistas which he opened particularly on the Renaissance and the European Enlightenment.

But as closely as his historical and philosophical studies were intertwined, the unity of his many interests is to be found in the philosophical conviction that man can participate in a higher order of life only through the realization of the perennial forms of human thought. He drew these philosophical conclusions most clearly in his great *Erkenntnistheorie* and in his *Philosophie der symbolischen Formen*. Cassirer's writings mirror far more than do those of most of his German colleagues his unusual gift as a teacher. He had a unique facility for clear and logical exposition, and all the products of his pen display his extraordinary sense of balance and aesthetic form. His capacity to project himself into the psychological and mental environment of a past age or of an individual thinker of the past did not make him forget the individual needs of a present-day audience or student. His understanding of human nature made him take his listeners or pupils as seriously as the philosophical and historical subjects he tried to expound to them. These qualities explain his success as a teacher in Germany, in Sweden, and in America.

Cassirer gave up his professorship in Hamburg when the Hitlerites came to power in Germany. This was natural, considering that he was one of the chief exponents of that liberal tradition of German thought which the Nazis tried to destroy by all means. But, being at the same time a Jew, he had to take refuge in foreign countries. No German was as deeply steeped in the German cultural tradition and very few had contributed so much to its growth within his generation as Ernst Cassirer. Many other German scholars who found themselves in a similar situation preferred to cut all their ties with their Jewish origin. Prior to Hitler not very many Germans would have criticized anyone for doing just that; on the contrary, many would have applauded such an attitude. Actually, Cassirer's unwillingness to abandon his Jewish faith proved a handicap in his earlier academic career, but he was too honest to dissimulate his heritage. He was also conscious that a great deal of his moral integrity and intellectual strength had come to him through his Jewish culture. Nor did this make him feel suspicious or bitter. There was little of Heinrich Heine in him, but much more of Felix Mendelssohn, to whom he can be compared in many respects. As Mendelssohn helped to discover for the Germans some of the greatest treasures of their cultural past, and at the same time contributed by his own creative work to the continuation of their classic tradition, so did Cassirer in the philosophic field.

Yet Cassirer's life and work do not belong to Germany alone. The philosophical revival of the last third of the nineteenth century was not merely a German event. It had its parallels and found its students in many lands, e.g., in the Italy of Benedetto Croce and to a lesser, though considerable, degree in modern French philosophy or in the Spain of Ortega y Gassett, from where it recently has spread far over Latin America. Among his German contemporaries, Cassirer was probably the one most conscious of the international significance of philosophy. Certainly he was the one German philosopher of distinction who had least indulged in construing the Kantian and post-Kantian German philosophy as a complete refutation of the philosophy of Western European Enlightenment. While German philosophers and historians were prone to describe the Kantian philosophy as a separation of the superior German from Western European civilization, Cassirer was always mindful of the fact that Kant had his roots in the Western European Enlightenment, or for that matter, that it was impossible to think of Goethe without Shaftesbury and Spinoza. These were some of the reasons which made him approach Western European thought with the same warmth of understanding which he showed in his German studies. He deserved the respect and affection of the philosophers of other countries which they showed him so often. Never did scholars of so many lands cooperate in expressing their admiration for a colleague of theirs as happened in the symposium on *History and Philosophy,* which the Oxford Press presented to him at his sixtieth birthday.

His knowledge of other civilizations, his truly cosmopolitan outlook, and the friendships which he acquired among his American colleagues and students, made the years of his exile not only bearable but fruitful. Others of his age never again came into their own after being separated from the world in which they had spent the major part of their life.

No doubt the events cast a tragic shadow over the last years of his career, but they did not change his fundamental beliefs, nor even his joy in research and teaching. The core of his personality was unaffected. He was unassuming and undemanding. His greatest satisfaction lay in giving others knowledge and wisdom.

PANORAMA OF 21 CIVILIZATIONS

THERE HAVE BEEN good days for those whose innocent self-assurance could produce simple formulas dressed in an imposing literary and academic gown. Arnold J. Toynbee does not belong to these simplifiers, despite the clamor of popular acclaim which has for the last few months engulfed this scholarly writer in our own enthusiastic country. Toynbee's learning is overwhelming, his style highly sophisticated, and his presentation of the course of history no easy summary from which facile conclusions could be drawn. His readers have to follow him far into the details and complexities of the life of civilizations, and an understanding is achieved only through the contemplation of the huge panorama of universal history.

Yet Toynbee, whose devoted followers here and in England could, before this year, have been counted perhaps in the hundreds, has been acclaimed in this country as the master seer who holds the key to the riddle of history. For four months the United States has been Toynbee-conscious. An astute advertising campaign for the new abridgment of his work, lectures in academic halls to overflow audiences the like of which has not been seen for years, laudatory reviews, articles in leading periodicals, have made Toynbee well known to the reading public of America. The Luce enterprises have adopted Toynbee; *Time* magazine lavished on him no less than eleven columns and a cover portrait.

The campaign was as surprising as it was unexpected. Basic to it perhaps was the hunger of a crisis-ridden people for the satisfactions of an orderly view of history. American historians do not begrudge Toynbee his sudden fame; yet as always on those rare occasions when a scholarly work achieves a wide popular acceptance there has been the danger of distortion and oversimplification. As yet, Toynbee has not received the serious critical attention he deserves. To convey adequately the structure and approach of this rich and complex work is impossible within the confines of the conventional short book review. It is the purpose of the writer to analyze and criticize the main points of Toynbee's *A Study of History* largely for those who already have some knowledge of the historian's work. But even here a brief rendition of Toynbee's thesis must be attempted in passing, a rendition which will, again, suffer inevitably from oversimplification.

Toynbee is no historian of the ivied walls. Foreign Office expert on the Near East during the First World War, reporter of the Greco-Turkish War, and more recently director of the Royal Institute of International Affairs and editor of its annual *Survey of International Affairs,* for over thirty years Toynbee has watched from an unparalleled vantage point the development of current history, while constantly adding to his knowledge of the past in reading. The result, more as a by-product of his career than anything else, has been his unique theory of civilizations.

Twenty-one civilizations, such as the Western, Hellenic, Egyptiac, Hittite, Indic, Sinic, Mexic, Yucatec, form Toynbee's field of historical study. Fourteen of these are dead, though some have left "fossilized relics" behind. Civilizations have come into being only during the last six thousand years, a small beat of time considering that human life commenced a few hundred thousand years ago. Therefore all civilizations are viewed by Toynbee as contemporaneous for philosophical purposes and taken to be parallel attempts of humanity to rise beyond primitivism.

This proposition has its merits. But Toynbee's interpretation has its pitfalls, too. He defines civilization as the smallest intelligible unit of historical study. Historic England, for example, cannot be understood unless attention is first focused on the whole of Western civilization of which she has formed an integral part. On the other hand a knowledge of Russian or even of Hellenic civilization is not needed in this connection. It is true that all surviving civilizations are living together today in a worldwide political and economic system, but their true being lies in their cultural individuality, which makes contacts like those between the Western and Russian civilizations rather ephemeral.

By conceiving of civilizations as self-contained entities Toynbee moves close to Spengler's theory of history whereby history repeats its inexorable cycle in one culture after another. Toynbee does not, however, consider civilizations as organisms which grow and lose their life-like plants. It is rather the idea of the Spenglerian "soul of a culture" which seems reflected in Toynbee's *Study*. For to him the real historical development is a spiritual process altogether. Political and social events are mere ripples on the surface of a stream that moves with a mighty drift invisible to the naked eye. The *élans* that produce civilizations are spiritual forces which Toynbee describes either in terms of Bergsonian philosophy or in New Testament words ("they are all seeds by the same Sower").

Still, in Toynbee's interpretation of history there is an uncertainty which in a way seems to mirror the mind of the author, who is at the same time both a mystic and a scholar proud of the capacity of the human intellect. It is clear that he feels that faith is the only power which moves mountains and the basic force in creating and sustaining civilizations. The age of Thucydides, Plato, Aristotle, for example, is not given by him any recognition as a great period. But he assumes in many places of his work that the rise of civilization required the solution of some vital technological problems or in other words the application of reason.

A similar approach can be discovered when we turn from what Toynbee calls the response to the natural environment to the response to the human environment. Although he emphasizes vigorously that we are dealing here no longer with the macrocosmos but with a microcosmos of human relations where only qualitative judgments should be in order, he cannot quite dispense with one quantitative factor. The *élan* that carries civilizations forward is not a momentum of enduring life, but an amount of energy which will be used up in a long series of responses to challenges. This conception is not identical but to some degree analogous with the Spenglerian idea of the inevitable death of civilizations.

Otherwise every effort is made to exclude any reference to biological cycles and to construe the birth, life, and death of civilizations as a struggle in the human soul. The disconcerting thought creeps up, however, that civilizations still in prime spiritual condition have been challenged and murdered by a human enemy who merely possessed greater power and in particular better technological weapons, as in the case of the Spanish conquest of the Incas. His humaneness and trust in the inner motivation of history make Toynbee shy away from drawing drastic conclusions about these fatalities of history. In general he is inclined to argue that such civilizations had already broken down and that the enemy applied only the *coup-de-grâce*.

Toynbee's civilizations are virtually self-contained units. They cannot learn from each other except in death. Once the initial obstacles of nature are overcome the growth of a civilization becomes an internal affair. Since civilization is a process of self-articulation through its individual members, Toynbee argues that history is made by great individuals, among them in the first place religious leaders, and by creative minorities. The mass adopts their ideas and manners by sheer emulation. But a special power of persuasion is required to convince the mass to part with traditional customs. The leaders acquire it by withdrawing for a time from active participation in the communal life. This motion leads to an "etherialization" of their moral and intellectual personalities which enables them to teach their fellow men after their return.

"Withdrawal-and-return" is, therefore, after "challenge-and-response" the second "law" of history. It is fairly well applicable to a long series of prophets and religious leaders. With regard to intellectual and political leaders it is of more questionable value. Wisely, some of the examples given by Toynbee in the more extensive version of his work have not been repeated in the Somervell edition. Did, for example, some of the greater monarchs, like Louis XIV, ever have an opportunity of withdrawing? But the concept becomes more doubtful when it is used to define the position of the leading nations at various periods of history. Athens did not "withdraw" from Hellenic society prior to assuming her great role in the Hellenic-Persian War after 480 B.C. She was pushed into the sea by the invasion of Xerxes and returned as the leading naval power of Greece.

The breakdown of civilizations, as already intimated, is, according to Toynbee, chiefly the result of the decline of the creativity in the creative minority which then turns into a "dominant" minority. As a consequence the masses cease to emulate the minority and the society begins to split open into various classes while losing at the same time its appeal to the unconverted "barbarians" outside. An "internal" and an "external" proletariat come into existence. (Toynbee defines "proletariat" as people "in" but not "of the society.") The "times of troubles" begin in which the dominant minority turns militaristic, and may try to build a universal state, though both philosophers and administrators may follow a nobler task. The external proletariat will form war bands whereas the internal proletariat will devote itself to the building of a universal church. If the society enters the stage of full disintegration, the collaboration of the internal and external proletariat will produce a new civilization carried on by the external proletariat but with the faith bequeathed upon it by the internal proletariat of the old society. It is at this point that the separate character of civilizations break down: a rib is taken from the old to form the backbone of the new civilization.

In the opinion of the reviewer Toynbee's theories of history suffer from taking their clue almost exclusively from the collapse of the Roman Empire. Even with regard to the latter event Toynbee's construction bypasses many fundamental problems. Strangely enough, the greatness of the Roman Empire receives no praise by the distinguished citizen and scholar of the British Empire. Rome's capacity to create law and unity in a chaotic world was her own genius, and it seems arbitrary to disregard her contribution and see in her history a senescent continuation of Hellenic life. The interaction between civilizations is far greater than Toynbee is willing to admit. It is also not confined to the religious heritage through a process of "affiliation" or "apparentation," but includes the social and political organizations which are an essential element of the real and ideal existence of any civilization. Historical challenges do not become merely "internal" and the affair of a creative minority, once a civilization has gotten under way.

Toynbee's *A Study of History* is strictly speaking not a philosophy of history. Modern philosophy of history, as represented among others by thinkers like Dilthey, Croce, Ortega y Gasset, or in England by R. G. Collingwood, has been chiefly concerned with the questions of historical knowledge itself. How can we gain a valid knowledge of the past while being ourselves only representatives of a passing moment in history? What methods does the historian employ to transcend the limitations of his subjective imagination and to achieve an objective view of history?

Toynbee seems not affected by these modern ideas. He does not entertain any doubt that the human mind is perfectly capable of correctly reconstructing the past. He states that there are three different methods of presenting the objects of our thought, and among them, the phenomena of human life. "The first is the ascertainment and recording of 'facts'; the second is the elucidation, through a comparative study of the facts ascertained, of general 'laws'; the third is the artistic re-creation of the facts in the form of 'fiction.'" He asserts that the first is the technique of history, the second that of science, while the third represents the technique of the drama and the novel. Soon he begins to tear down these distinctions between the techniques of history, anthropology, and fiction which he himself had first advanced. He fails, however, to analyze the actual nature of "facts" and "laws." Instead we are only told that the novel and drama contained good history, while history on its part was using fiction to select, arrange, and present its facts. Moreover, not only anthropology but also history is now supposed "to make a beginning with the formulation of laws."

Such statements are not apt to create a firm philosophical foundation for the author's ambitious project nor do they enable the reader to grasp its full intentions. All through his work Toynbee maintains that he is merely applying the inductive method. To him facts are ready-made objective elements which through an imaginative interpretation can be woven into wider patterns. By a comparative study of these structures laws can be discovered. However, the role of the imagination is both greater and smaller than Toynbee assumes. History is the re-enactment of the past in the mind of the historian, and even "facts" exist only there. But in contrast to poetry they call for critical verification. Even less can imagination by itself produce an objective selection and arrangement of facts. To assert the contrary would necessitate the identification of the historical novel with critical historical writing as well as of mythology with universal history. In this respect Toynbee tends to neglect not only the modern philosophical exploration of the problems of historical research but even the critical demands which Thucydides first laid down.

It is Herodotus' rather than Thucydides' spirit which hovers over Toynbee's book. It displays the same truly catholic scope, the same boundless curiosity for the phenomenal world and the delight in its literary presentation, while methodological problems receive scant attention. But the parallel should not be overdone. One could say also that his work renewed the great tradition of the Christian philosophy of history which dominated Western thought from Augustine to Bossuet, if this view of history had not rested upon the belief that divine rather than human actions constituted the only objects worthy of speculation. Toynbee remains a humanist, and though he knows of higher hopes, the achievements of man constitute the proper subjects of research.

By focusing attention upon the methodology and philosophy of Toynbee's study the full scope of his intellectual achievement is not adequately presented. The work is woven like a rich carpet with impressive patterns in deep, if dark, colors. It breaks away in earnest from the historiography which centers around a single nation or a single civilization, and with its wealth of information and literary illustration opens entirely new vistas of history. It is history, philosophically interpreted, rather than a philosophy of history, written by a devout visionary possessed by great poetic gifts. Attempts have already been made to turn his book into a shibboleth in the ideological war that is raging. But the work of this truly gentle mind is not belligerent. It can be said with confidence that it succeeds in looking far over the world of universal history, though it is often satisfied with mere aesthetic contemplation at the expense of sharp philosophical and historical analysis.

THE SOCIAL BASIS OF
THE GERMAN REFORMATION

ONE OF THE intrinsic weaknesses of our historical studies is
that we can understand the past only by utilizing analogies
to our age. What we comprehend of past events or personalities most readily is the features which they seem to have in
common with our own forms of life, and it is from these associ-
ations that we take our cue in exploring the past. We know
how fallacious this method can be, since a closer study of the
historical landscape possibly reveals that what we regarded
as a landmark had actually little significance in its own age
and what we believed a resemblant factor was nothing but a
superficial similarity. So we have very often to burn the
bridges over which we entered into the territory of the past.

This applies particularly to sociological methods in history.
They are delusive if used as an absolute criterion or without
historical sense, that is, by not making allowance for the differences of historical societies. And if we look at the studies of
social life in the sixteenth century, we shall find that the gulf
that separates the social life of the nineteenth and twentieth
centuries from that of the sixteenth has often been too easily
bridged over (cf. for example Roy Pascal, *The Social Basis of
the German Reformation*, London, 1933). A great deal of
work will have to be spent on re-examining our general
conceptions and on a new reading and uncovering of source

material before we shall obtain an adequate picture of the social situation of Germany at the beginning of the sixteenth century. That is a prerequisite for a true evaluation of the influence which social conditions had on the Reformation.

We stand on firm ground as far as the knowledge of economic history is concerned. The work of the last two or three generations of economists and historians has endowed us with a knowledge of the history of German trade, commerce, and industry in the later Middle Ages and in early modern times which enables us to follow the great changes in that sphere with little difficulty. Even the study of agrarian conditions, which for a time did not keep pace with the research done on capitalism, has advanced and produced more definite and reliable results. But in estimating the impact of these economic factors upon the structure of society we are still in an exploratory stage. Two points especially should be given more careful attention.

First, the scholars—and a great number of most able ones made the economic and social change of the sixteenth century the field of their study—approached their subject largely with a view to inquiring into the origins of modern capitalism. Consequently, they were more interested in the advent of fresh changes as such than in the average conditions of that particular age. They treated the economic history of the sixteenth century as a prelude to the present-day system of economy and hence were prone to overemphasize all that seemed to indicate a breaking away from the older economic system. Yet it is doubtful whether the rise of early capitalism in Germany actually revolutionized German society as a whole. We observe the growth of finance and large-scale trade and new forms of industrial organization chiefly in Upper Germany, whereas Middle and North Germany preserved the traditional habits of agrarian society. For the bulk of Germany the sixteenth century did not bring forth a considerable change in economic conditions, the revolution of prices perhaps being the only experience in which the nation as a whole participated. With this single, though of course important, exception we may say that North Germany, the birthplace of Lutheranism and future stronghold of Protestantism, was not witnessing a considerable transformation of economic life during the sixteenth century. The economic constitution of these sections of Germany had been established considerably earlier and nothing sensational was to happen for a long time to come. The South of Germany was going through an age of profound transformation of its economic status, but the period of bold achievements and successful enterprises was superseded by an epoch of deterioration and contraction. In space as well as in time the rise of capitalism in Germany is distinctly limited. The era of the Fuggers marks a new departure in the general economic history of Europe, but in German history little more than a glamorous episode.

But if it is true that the influence of the new capitalistic enterprises on the general life of the people should not be overrated, it becomes even more urgent to differentiate German society of the sixteenth century from modern society. That leads us to a second aspect of principal significance. We are too much accustomed to such convenient class divisions as feudal, upper, middle, and lower classes and to conceiving the social relationship of these groups in analogy to the structure of modern society. Recent sociological studies have taught us that these classifications do not suffice to understand social actions and reactions in our society; they are, moreover, even less appropriately applied to the social life of the sixteenth century. There was a greater variety of social groups than the three or four classes into which we usually divide society today. More essential, however, is the discrepancy of the underlying social principles. The terms upper, middle, and lower classes are taken from the stratification of an acquisitive society, a type of human society in which property and income confer a definite social rank upon its members.

Medieval society, however, was built on different principles. The order of feudal ranks was in theory constructed not on the pattern of income and property but according to functional duties. We know, to be sure, that the authority which was wielded for the good of society was endowed with material wealth, particularly with income from ground rents. But since ground rents could not be accumulated, a kind of social superiority developed which was very different from what we see in modern society. In the sixteenth century this system of medieval feudalism was in decay; landed property had become convertible into capital wealth and vice versa. But a great importance was still attached to landed property, which still bestowed on its holders certain political prerogatives, and the new rich were therefore very eager to join the ranks of the landed aristocracy.

Medieval society, furthermore, was not only feudal but religious in a way that made itself felt in the social structure. Again we are aware that the Church fell victim to feudalism, but the fact nevertheless remains that it possessed a sense of social honor and distinction quite at variance with feudal classification. The struggle between Church and state, emperor and pope had forced the Church to become a political power, and it was this development which forced the Church to approve of and to participate in feudal organization. Yet though the Church's servants and its head became feudal lords and in the later Middle Ages capitalists, the Church showed itself able to call into existence a group of people who took their stand outside a society organized on the lines of rich and poor.

Again and again the demand had been renewed which Christ made upon his followers to live in poverty and to seclude themselves from the temptations of the world. The Church preached this belief and, on the other hand, made use of it for political purposes. In order to have at its disposal a body of true servants and independent officials, it tried to separate its priests from the rest of the flock not by giving them social advantages but by taking away social rights. All these attempts, like forcing celibacy upon the clergy and asking for abstention from property, succeeded only for a time.

But they were not fruitless. If we compare the endeavors of the secular lords to build up a corps of state officials with the parallel attempts of the Church, it is quite obvious that the Church reaped a better harvest. The majority of the clergy failed in their duties; yet there were not only individual saints but a large group of priests and monks who conceived their task not as a private occupation but as a functional commission.

But what did this mean for the structure of society? The priests and monks were socially disenfranchised in order to gain at once higher social dignity. To take up the humble life of a monk was meritorious in itself. However paradoxical to attach social dignity to a renunciation of society, such holy conduct could not be divested of social significance. It was always uncertain what place priests and monks would exactly claim in the scale of social ranks. Little doubt, however, was voiced that they deserved a high station.

Thus, in addition to the importance of landed property, a second principle became valid which is opposed to the life of modern society, or at least to what modern economists mostly describe as such. Within a society which was not originally founded on property and income, though already in a state of transformation toward such an organization, there still existed groups which derived their social distinction from their social detachment, from the idea of service to the whole.

It was very important that during the later Middle Ages this idea of service underwent a change. Service to the Church was the aim in the beginning, now it became service to the community of which the clergyman happened to be a member. Church and state came closer together in the fourteenth and fifteenth centuries, the State gaining control over many departments of Church life. The clergy, on the other hand, obtained a new hold over the life of the larger classes. Besides many deplorable results as revealed in the abundance of superstitious miracles and similar phenomena, we find that what was best in the thought and practice of the clergy and monasteries kindled the flame of true Christian enthusiasm among the laity. The "brotherhoods of common life" stand out as an example of how the realization of Christian principles among the clergymen and monks awakened the laymen to emulate them and partake in their works of prayer and love and in their renunciation of outward distinction.

The influence of these movements of reform in the fourteenth and fifteenth centuries was varying. These centuries were full of reform movements within and without the Church. We see that in many cases the movements resulted in putting at the disposal of the Roman Church a group of people who saw their task in mere zeal for the pope. I mention the Dominicans and their role in building up the Inquisition. And again in spite of all the examples of stupidity and brutality of which we know, I cannot find that the revival of this ardor can be traced merely to selfishness and economic interests. The work done in more recent years, chiefly by Catholic scholars in Germany, has convinced me that the old Church still commanded a great number of irreproachable and able preachers and theologians.

But there was a second group of reformers who did not join the struggle for the restoration of papal authority, but instead began to apply the ideal of apostolic poverty to the Church itself, demanding that not a single class but the Church as a whole live in poverty. This view appealed to many people as early as the beginning of the Franciscan movement, and the Church had generally a hard task to reconcile the tendencies of the mendicant orders with its own compromising attitude toward social problems. The Church never quite succeeded. The ideal of apostolic poverty most forcefully preached by St. Francis, the son of a rich merchant, resounded throughout Christendom. It was carried on in the monasteries and among laymen, and it was eventually supported by the rising states which wanted to exclude the Church from all secular affairs. Thus the religious ideal became a political claim as well. The conflict between Church and state, now renewed on a different level, gave new opportunities to the clergy. Henceforth we meet more often in history with the undesirable type of theologians who proved themselves submissive to all demands of secular government. But there were others who used the tension which existed between state and Church in order to assert the Christian ideals in criticizing both forces. They received support from their bishops or from the princes and magistrates or whoever might show himself readiest to lend assistance to the priest who wanted to fulfill his task within his assigned community.

The tension between state and Church, as it appeared in the fifteenth and at the beginning of the sixteenth centuries, gave the clergy an opportunity to play a more independent part in society. In countries like England and France, where the state had already been centralized to a comparatively high degree and the authority of the central government could make itself felt throughout the nation, even a reformed clergy could not assume command of affairs, since the government was able to remove the tension by bargaining with or fighting against the papacy. In both countries it was more a change of institutions than of faith that took place in the first half of the sixteenth century. The religious reformation of these countries began in the course of later social and political upheavals, a development that was to connote an episode in French and an epoch in English history.

The situation in Germany was unique. The pressure of the decadent Roman Church bore heavily on the whole people, for no other country had so many just grievances against the Roman see. On the other hand, not only was Germany divided into many territories, but the governmental authority of the territorial states was comparatively weak. No territorial prince could hope to carry through a thorough reformation of the Church. He necessarily feared his neighbors and his subjects who were still bound to the Roman Church. Since the way of political reform of the Empire was blocked, only a religious principle could open the way into the future. A principle, however, was of little use unless it was made vital by a group of people who enjoyed the confidence of various classes because of their devotion to a higher cause than the pursuit of economic interests. An earnest preacher who lived up to the ideals which he proclaimed was still exercising an enormous authority in Germany. He was remote from the daily struggle for social hegemony, his office was functional and reflected a higher unity of human relations for which people most ardently longed.

If we consider what channels of influencing society were at the disposal of the clergy, we can understand the responsibility which the clerical office carried with it. Theologians were the only men who knew Latin, except for the small though increasing groups of educated people like jurists and humanists, and they were the people who had to read pamphlets and books before the laity, even when the publication of books in the vernacular had become a common feature. In the fifteenth and early sixteenth centuries the clergy were holding an almost absolute monopoly of information, and there is little doubt that the agitation of the common people before and after the appearance of Luther was effected chiefly through clerics.

Now we come to the problem of Luther. I do not see the slightest possibility of ascribing the origins of Luther's reformation to a particular social class in the sense that his theology was a rationalization of existing class interests. His father was of peasant stock and had become a miner and ultimately made a moderate fortune. The son could look forward to attaining a higher social status by studying law, when his sudden conversion to monkish life led him far away from all thoughts of a social career. It seems to me absurd to read any social feeling into the development of Luther's religious experiences and conceptions. Like all great religious prophecies they came to maturity in a mind ready to withdraw from the life of the world and not bent on world dominance.

But at least medieval society had given room to these searchers for truth and grace, and monasticism had become an acknowledged institution. It is very important that Luther attained his new religious insight as a monk and not as an outsider to the Church. His earnest strife for attaining the highest ideals of the Church gave him the strength to set up a higher goal. And being a member of the Church, he was seeking reform of the Church and not a revolt against her tradition.

But the special structure of society in the fifteenth century was auspicious for what was going to happen. The University of Wittenberg, like most of the German universities of that age, enjoyed comparatively more freedom of teaching than the old Church universities. Founded in the capital of a territory by a secular prince, the University of Wittenberg was not so closely under the control of the Church authorities. It was here that Luther as professor of the Holy Scriptures began to lecture on his new conception of Christian faith. Most probably he was not aware of his audacity; it seemed but natural to him that professors should not simply expound the law of the Church but contribute by their work and thinking to its reformation. A new conception of academic office revealed itself here which can be fully explained only by reverting to the particular situation of society. To conceive of the professors as the living conscience of the Church, instead of as simply executing its rulings, was an unthinkable idea in the heyday of the Middle Ages. It shows that these reforming clerics conceived of their functional authority in a much wider sense than before. They had originally derived their authority from the Church for the good of the Church. But now they applied it to the Church itself, to a Church which had become hopelessly entangled in worldly affairs, while they had kept a certain aloofness from secular life.

Perhaps, on the other hand, they knew the life of the laity better than the Church government, although certainly not the political or business life. They alone were aware of the deep

desire of individuals of all ranks to embrace the Christian life
and obtain inward peace.

They had brought the gospel to the rising classes, they had
kept the fire in all divisions of society. But now they got into
a serious conflict between their prior mandate and the confidence that their congregations had thrust upon them. Luther
started his controversy over indulgences which was to drag
him into the worldwide arena, in the course of the difficulties
which had arisen within his congregation. He became the
Protestant reformer because he wanted to maintain the dignity
of the clerical office. That added fresh power to his strength
in those moments of weakness when an inner voice was warning him that a single man could not pretend to be wiser than
the *consensus saeculorum*.

Thus the realization of functional authority as accomplished
by the Roman Church proved of great importance even in the
inner life of the man who was to abolish monasticism and
priesthood. But even greater was the significance for the first
expansion of Lutheran ideas. We have no book on Protestantism comparable to the scope of Harnack's *History of the Mission and Expansion of the Christian Church in the First Three
Centuries*. But toward such an analysis, it may be said at least
that it forms an outstanding characteristic of the first phase
of the Reformation period that from Luther to Thomas Mün-
tzer all Church reformers who entered the battle came from
the ranks of monks or priests.

In the light of what has been said, this phenomenon can be
more easily expounded. These reformers lived in the same
conflict of duty to the Church and to the people as did Luther.
They were therefore prepared to follow the path that Luther
showed, and so they made public the new truth to all the
classes of the people. It was they who awakened overnight
the enthusiasm of the people and from that great achievement
we may learn how strong was their authority over the masses.
This authority was not due to the conformity of the clergy to
the existing social stratification but to its independence. Since

they derived their social honor not from feudal or property privileges, they appeared as more objective and reliable leaders, as the best fitted intermediaries between the classes of society. Whether this clerical group, which was a small minority within a much wider class, lived up to the expectations of the people, I do not wish to discuss. That question belongs to the history of the period in which the Protestant churches constituted themselves as new social units. It is, however, obvious that the Protestant reformers were in a position to form their original social program without much consideration of special class interests.

I have attempted to demonstrate three things. First, a problem of the method of approach: the stratification of our modern society should not be expected to offer much help for the understanding of other ages. The directing principles on which the society of the later Middle Ages was founded are at variance with those of our age. Second, a closer study of the society of the fifteenth and sixteenth centuries shows that the idea of the monk's calling was still a potent force which was embodied in a number of powerful personalities. Third, it was this minority that used the opportunity to assert its unifying religious ideas against and amidst conflicting economic interests. To this cause the strength and the rapid spread of the German Reformation in its first years can be largely traced. There was no one-sided social basis of the origins of the German Reformation, but there was a particular constellation of social groups and social factors which was auspicious for the cause of reform. The most fortunate result was the fact that Protestantism as a religious idea was not from its very inception bound up with a distinct class interest.

POWER POLITICS AND CHRISTIAN ETHICS
IN EARLY GERMAN PROTESTANTISM*

THE ASSERTION THAT modern German power politics had its
roots in the rise of Lutheranism has often been pronounced
in recent times. In my opinion such a proposition must be rejected. There can be no question that twentieth-century German imperialism had sources far back in German history. It
is also true that the German Protestantism of the nineteenth
and twentieth centuries carries a heavy responsibility for the
untrammeled growth of power politics. But modern German
Protestantism was far removed from the Lutheranism of the
period 1517–1648. It was warped by ideas not germane to
its original heritage and wed to a political and social reality
vastly different from the conditions of sixteenth-century Germany. A true insight into the nature of our problem can be
gained only if we look from the sixteenth century forward
instead of drawing conclusions from viewing the past in the
light of the present.

Luther's religion was based on the transcendental experience of the individual whom the Word of God had reached
and transformed. This fundamental conception had led him
step by step to oppose not only the core of Roman Catholic
theology but also the politico-ecclesiastic institutions of the

* This paper was originally presented to the International Congress of
Historical Sciences in Stockholm, August 24, 1960.

world into which he was born. According to Luther the Christian Church as it appeared on earth was not the simple representation of the kingdom of God nor was the pope the vicar of Christ who together with the priesthood administered the treasure of grace acquired by Christ's death for the benefit of the faithful in their search for salvation. Luther also denied that the visible Church possessed the divine wisdom with which to judge the political actions of men. He tore the unity of the *ecclesia militans* and *triumphans* asunder. The true Church, the communion of saints, to which the true Christian belonged, was to him an invisible and metaphysical entity surpassing the ages. True Christians were, and always would be, a minority. Luther refused to build a visible Church by assembling these few, because there were no clear criteria for distinguishing good Christians from pseudo-Christians. But even more important was the consideration that the Word of God was to reach everybody, and it was for that reason that the true Christian, in obedience to God and in love of his weak neighbor, had to accept a general Church. This Church was not unrelated to the true invisible Church. Wherever the Word of God was correctly preached and the sacraments properly administered, the Church visible and invisible temporarily merged.

The visible Church of Luther, which he himself hesitated to call "Church" and preferred to call *"gemeine,"* had no authority to lay down the law in political affairs. On the contrary, Luther called in the secular authority to organize and maintain the Church of the pure doctrine. Secular authority, *Obrigkeit,* or the state, like the visible Church, was a God-willed institution. Man was evil and if not forced to be orderly would exterminate the few true Christians and make the preaching of the Word of God impossible. But by taming the human beast the state did not become a Christian state since it was beyond its capacity to turn men into Christians and was employing violence, which was incompatible with Christian love. All Christians, however, owed the State strict obedience and even unjust actions of princes or tyrants had to be patiently suffered as God's penalties upon sinful men. Only in matters of religious conscience was the individual bound to express his conviction, but he had to be prepared to accept martyrdom for it. The order of this world could not be transformed into a Christian order, since it was only of a transitory nature and of no real significance compared to eternity, to which the individual had no other access but faith.

In their application to actual politics these ideas of Luther tended to elevate all existing political authority and to what extremes he could carry his principles was demonstrated by his attitude toward the Peasants' War. It should be emphasized, however, that the *"weltliche Obrigkeit"* which Luther had in mind was not the omnipotent state of the eighteenth century, let alone subsequent developments, but the weak territorial state of sixteenth-century Germany in which power was divided between princes and estates. In questions on which the two agreed—and this meant chiefly holding the lower classes in place—Lutheranism added further strength to social conservatism. But politically early Lutheranism did relatively little to end the division of power within the *Ständestaat* and this was to prove a continuing handicap for strong internal and external policies of the princes.

The studies on the distribution of the secularized Church goods in Germany are inadequate. But it can be said that both princes and noblemen profited from the despoliation of the old Church. In addition to property the noblemen acquired rights, such as those of patrons of local churches and parishes, that gave them considerable influence on the Church regime. Yet on balance the princes made greater material and moral gains. Their new resources helped to finance the military exertions which some of them made between 1525 and 1555. But for the future it was even more important that as *summi episcopi* of the new territorial churches they added a quasi-spiritual function to their princely dignity. It is true that the episcopal function was construed as an obligation and not as

a right, but this distinction made little difference for the enhanced popular prestige of their princes, the more so since
through the assumption of the canonic jurisdiction and the
direction of schools and social welfare the scope of princely
activity was greatly expanded.

In these and related developments the foundation was laid
for the rise of the princes over the estates. But the advent of
absolutism was a slow process and still other than Lutheran
influences contributed to its rise. As a matter of fact the first
German states in which the power of the estates was broken
were Catholic Bavaria and Austria.

It has been necessary to discuss the impact of Lutheranism
on the emergence of absolute princely power, since the arrival
of absolutism has often been declared the real cause of bold
schemes of power politics. Absolutism and power politics cannot be so closely identified. But it is true that in the history of
the Continent during the seventeenth and eighteenth centuries
the achievement of absolute princely authority, or as it was
then called "sovereignty," was practically always the prerequisite for an expansionist policy or was even gained
through an activist foreign policy. The term "power politics,"
originally formed for political polemics, does not lend itself
easily to an objective treatment of history. The term can be
defined only in a relative way, since no policy exists without
the ultimate, if latent, sanction of force. We shall speak of
power politics only in cases where the application of power
for self-aggrandizement tends to become an exclusive aim in
disregard of the rights and the well-being of the international
community and, as should be added, of the own people as
well.

Such trends were not very noticeable among the Lutheran
states of Germany prior to 1648. An obvious explanation
might be found in the fact that they were simply incapable
of generating the power necessary for big political adventures.
But we should not overlook that Brandenburg adopted an
activist policy after 1643 under conditions that looked for-

bidding. Moreover, while in the second half of the sixteenth century the individual Protestant states lacked sufficient strength, they could have formed a very considerable power if they had federated and acted in common. The fact that neither a Protestant league nor a single Protestant state attempted to enter the great power conflicts of Europe in force, must have had among others also religious reasons.

It has been argued—by some in condemnation, by others in praise—that by removing the control of the Church over the state, Luther restored the true life of the state that fed on power and could only be directed by practical reason. But this amounts to an identification of Luther and Machiavelli that is untenable. For the Italian humanist, in spite of his pessimistic view of human nature, the individual could achieve greatness only in the political arena and the reason that ruled politics was the highest wisdom attainable. Although Luther did not deny that reason made a difference between bad and good government, this reason was not even the shadow of the supreme truth of revelation, and even the greatest political triumphs were but idle pagan dreams. The state had only one divinely ordained task, the establishment of that elementary order that made the preaching of the Word of God possible. The administration of justice and the protection of pure doctrine consequently became the key principles of government in early Lutheranism. War was allowed only in defense, and even wars for the spread of true religion were declared sinful. Originally Luther was quite reluctant to accept the juristic theory that the Protestant princes had the right to resist the emperor, and in his early years he urged Christians to suffer the progress of the Turks as God's penalty for their sins.

In all these teachings there were no incentives for an activist foreign policy, not to speak of power politics. The individual prince who wished to be a Christian was counseled to consider his dignity not a personal possession but an office to be administered for the realization of God's supreme plan. Beyond this Luther suggested that a Christian prince ought to inject some Christian love into his practice of government by using a more humane equity instead of legalistic justice or even by accepting an injustice rather than retaliating by going to war.

Luther, who held a rather low opinion of the character of princes, did not really expect them to exercise such self-denial, and historians have failed to discover events that would refute his skepticism. Even with regard to the main body of Lutheran political principles Luther's critical judgment on the character of German princes, which contrasted so strangely to his extreme reverence for the princely office, seems to me largely borne out by the mass of the German princes. Few of them were very deeply and consciously motivated in their political and personal actions by Lutheran social ethics. It is true that such patriarchs as August I of Saxony, Christoph of Württemberg, William IV of Hesse, and John George of Brandenburg realized Lutheran ethics and through their concentration on the internal affairs of their territories greatly contributed to the well-being of their subjects. There were, however, many others who although abstemious in foreign activities failed to share the accruing benefits with their subjects. By and large the completely dissolute and profligate type seems to have been infrequent, and the flabby and politically more or less aimless figures filled the scene. In external affairs policy centered around martial alliances with a view to the future inheritance of additional territories. But this policy was counterbalanced by the widely continuing custom of partitioning the dynastic possessions among younger and elder sons. In addition efforts were made to install younger sons as Protestant administrators in neighboring bishoprics, efforts usually promoted through intrigues among the dynasties and the nobility represented on the chapters.

The fight for the survival of the Lutheran faith was conducted by the Protestant princes defensively with shrewd exploitation of the chaotic constitutional law of the Holy Roman Empire. That this fight would not be carried forward by a bold offensive was already settled in 1529. Philip of Hesse, the best political brains, though not the best political character in the first generation of Protestant princes, then tried to build a Protestant front that was to reach from Lübeck to Zurich. But the passionate adherence to the purity of doctrine made alliance and federation possible only among people of identical religious beliefs. Luther's stubborn refusal to accept Zwingli into the fold ended any attempt to create a grand alliance of German Protestantism that might have gained a dominant position in Germany and possibly even in Europe. The chance was blocked by Luther's religious decision and his theological ruling made it also thereafter impossible to develop policies which would have wrested the initiative from the Catholic opponents. The splits within German Protestantism subsequently were not only those between Lutheranism and Calvinism but occurred also within the Lutheran camp itself.

In contrast to the stagnation of all significant external activity in Lutheran Germany, Calvinism always displayed signs of political enterprise. Calvinism showed itself less bothered by certain theological scruples than Lutheranism and was imbued by its founder with an intense feeling for universal mission. Moreover, although Calvinism in its early forms was as otherworldly as Lutheranism, it demanded far-reaching reforms of the worldly order, as well as of the moral conduct of the individual. The Calvinist princes formed in the second half of the sixteenth century the party of movement in Germany. Yet they were hemmed in by Catholics and Lutherans. Only the revolt of the Netherlands improved their political stature, and the religious and intellectual ideas that spread from Holland proved influential even in Lutheranism. In 1613 the Brandenburg dynasty adopted the Calvinist faith. The consequences of this event were negligible under the Electors John Sigismund and George William, but a gate had been opened for the entry of those ideas that molded the personality of Frederick William, the Great Elector.

But the Calvinism that the Great Elector largely received from the Netherlands was a hybrid plant. It was permeated with the humanistic ideas that had revived in France and the Netherlands and that affected also personalities such as Gustavus Adolphus and Richelieu. The Neo-Stoic school produced ideals of man which were ascetic but gave man's action in the natural world a moral justification quite different from the teachings of early Calvinism and even more of orthodox Lutheranism. The state now became the chief arena in which the individual had to prove his value. As incompatible as Hugo Grotius and the writers of the "interests of state" or the *raison d'état* may appear, they all reflect the diminishing consciousness of the transitoriness of this world. In the light of the new philosophies the differences over pure Christian doctrine also lost their essential meaning.

German Lutheranism in its popular manifestations strongly resisted the new ideas and most passionately the "terrible animal *raison d'état*," but Lutheran doctrine of obedience to established authorities together with the new power of absolutist princes made it easy to muzzle such feelings. But while already the activist foreign policy of the Great Elector was enlivened by other than Lutheran ideas, the power politics of Frederick the Great belonged to an altogether different religious and philosophical age.

MISFORTUNE AND MORAL
DECISIONS IN GERMAN HISTORY

BY THE EVENTS of the year 1945, the Germans again came into possession of their own history. The Hitler regime deprived the Germans of the right freely to interpret their great and rich past. The National-Socialist "historical myth," a thin disguise for naked ideals of power, was an attempt to throttle completely the freedom of historical research, which is in fact one of the proudest achievements of modern German intellectual life. Essentially in order to cut off the Germans from the full inheritance of their own history, National-Socialism tried to prevent the critical understanding of German history. Only those events and ideas might be considered—and then only under artificial stage lighting—which could serve to prepare and to enhance Hitler's dictatorship and world rule. But, as a result, German history thereby was brought fundamentally into sharp contradiction with Western Christian development, of which it is but a part.

The freedom to take hold of the meaningful substance of German history through critical understanding and evaluation exists again, and it is the task of a new generation to make the best use of this opportunity. It is of the greatest interest that, in this opening stage, we should take heed of the voice of the revered and greatest living master of German historical research. I am pleased to accept an invitation to take part in the discussion opened by Friedrich Meinecke with an article in the October number of *Der Monat.*

It is understandable that German historians, on beginning reconstruction of the concept of German history, should be concerned lest their revision of historical valuations be taken for opportunistic adaptation to the new political powers of the hour, and therefore for renewed political submissiveness (*Gleichschaltung*). It is also understandable that precisely those who, in view of the aberrations of the Third Reich, continued to think critically concerning the course of German history, should, at the present moment, wish to avoid making a self-righteous show of their own foresight. After Hitler's war, like a mighty earthquake, ruined the German scene and the lives of millions of persons, it would be presumptuous for a single individual to come forward to prove how right he had been in the past.

If, however, one wishes to achieve a new interpretation of the major forces of German history one must not go too far in being concerned about appearing to be a new "joiner" (*"Gleichschalter"*). Any self-righteousness with reference to past differences of opinion is certainly out of place these days, but a radical historical criticism is one of the most urgent of national tasks to make it possible for the German people to understand its present lot and to devote its energy to the achievement of future objectives in keeping with the highest ideals of the German past. It is in this sense that a new awareness of historical continuity between Germany's past and present must be re-established. But this does not at all mean that we have to exculpate in any way the Germany of yesterday—Hitler's Germany—or the Germany of the day before yesterday—Bismarck's and William II's Germany. For in the thousand years of German history, each of these epochs constitutes still but a brief watch in the night.

Few speak directly of Nazi Germany, and few of the Weimar Republic either. The Empire of Bismarck and William II has become the center of discussion. Obviously, many see in the Third Reich an absolute perversion of the ideas on which Bismarck's Empire was founded. There is certainly some truth in this explanation. To a certain degree, Hitler did represent the intrusion of a foreigner into German history. He was indeed in a sense more distinctly a foreigner than the Corsican Napoleon was in France. Hitler's original political ideas, above all his racist theory, developed on the barren soil of the disintegrating Habsburg Empire. But he experienced for the first and only time a sense of belonging in the German army during the First World War, and in the disintegration of German society after the war he was able to make himself the master of German destiny.

For that reason it is not possible after all to consider Hitler as a "non-German" event, and Friedrich Meinecke, as a matter of fact, has always strictly avoided doing so. But it is also not right to see in the Third Reich the result of tragic accidents of an individual and a general kind. Tragedy certainly was not lacking, for it is always present in history, particularly at the great turning-points. For all that, Hitler's success in Germany between 1930 and 1943 would not have been possible without the acclamation, voluntary at first, which he received particularly from the German bourgeoisie. It was Bismarck who maintained the Prussian-German army above the constitution and prepared the German bourgeoisie to follow autocrats. It actually means little that the army, or more exactly the generals, eventually fared badly under Hitler, since hardly anyone was more responsible for the victory of the authoritarian over the popular conception of the state in Germany than the leaders of the Reichswehr. And there can be no question that the traditions of the Bismarckian Empire were the principal factor contributing to the destruction of the Weimar Republic.

Any historical contemplation of the past must begin with the assumption that the course of past history was determined by causes and motives which make this course explicable. If we did not believe in such logical explanations of history, historical research would cease to have meaning. But the recognition of the causes for the victory of one or another state which we may discover by retrospective analysis, should not prevent us from understanding history as the struggle between necessity and freedom. Ranke described freedom in history in these words: "We see before us a series of events following upon and determining each other. When I say, 'determine,' I do not mean, to be sure, by absolute necessity. The great thing is rather that everywhere human freedom is presupposed. History studies the scenes of freedom. This is its greatest appeal. But freedom is joined by force, indeed elemental force; without it, freedom would come to an end in secular events as well as in the world of ideas. At any moment again, something novel may originate that could be traced back only to the first and common source of all human action and inaction. Nothing exists merely for the sake of something else; nothing is wholly subsumed in the reality of something else. . . ."

Ranke was convinced that the free moral decision as well as intellectual and religious creativity of the single individual or people constituted fundamental elements of history. At many points in his work, Ranke reminded his readers that events might have taken another course had other factors come into play or other decisions been taken. On the other hand, Ranke did not hesitate to recognize a nemesis in history. We know that Ranke was very cautious in passing moral judgment and tended in general to harmonize the sharp conflicts of historical life. But he never questioned fundamentally the freedom of human action in the struggle with historical necessity.

If we were to consider by itself Friedrich Meinecke's article on "Wrong Paths in our History," and forget his critical observations elsewhere on German history, it would seem that he can see fundamentally few truly wrong paths, but essentially only paths of tragic misfortune in German history. The word "tragic" is in this case used in a very superficial sense as denoting the influence of external forces rather than the struggle of human hearts. Tragic guilt is not mentioned. The course of German history since 1648 is depicted as more or less inevitable. "It was the geopolitical position of Germany in the center of Europe which forced upon us the alternative either to remain a low pressure area or to become a power state," Meinecke declares in the decisive passage.

Now this is certainly true in the sense that Germany had a right to obtain the means of self-preservation, and it must also be admitted that in the eighteenth century this could only take place within the forms of despotism. I cannot see that Frederick the Great deserves the accusations made against him, particularly outside of Germany, though it must not be forgotten that they are to a large degree the result of the misuse of Old Fritz by modern German patriotism.

The first question which must be asked, in my opinion, is whether the power won by Germany since the days of Frederick was really used for simple self-preservation and for the pacification of Europe. Here it must be said that, since the middle of the nineteenth century, the feeling of common responsibility for Europe as a whole has been in rapid decline everywhere in Europe, but most particularly in Germany that, one would think, as the central country had a very special interest in the peaceful progress of the Continent. The central position of Germany, however, was utilized almost exclusively to justify power politics. Bismarck, who could speak with real scorn of Europe as a "mere geographic name," did show, for all that, some feeling for the prosperity of the whole European community of states. But the annexation of Alsace-Lorraine created lasting French-German tension, and Bismarck's peacefully intended alliance policy was accompanied by bellicose language and constant increase of armaments. Under William II, Germany turned quickly to the open sea of world politics. In the First World War, the leaders of German militarism and heavy industry found themselves easily joined in adventurous expansionist plans, and the forces of moderate opposition were repressed without great difficulty by them.

This brings us directly to the second problem, which is the domestic leadership of the state in modern Germany, or the vain struggle for genuine liberalization and democratization of German political forms. I hear two principal objections to this thesis, first, that the democratic movement of 1848— 49 might have become more nationalist than the authoritarian governments, and second, that a democratic government would have sapped the power of German self-preservation. It cannot be questioned that modern mass democracy carries within it all the elements of radical nationalism. Jingoism and chauvinism have always raised their heads anew in Western democracy, but also have always been thrust back within bounds by the American, English, and French nations. And the greatest democratic movement of Germany, the old Social-Democracy, did not prove to be a chauvinist force in German history.

With regard to the argument that German foreign policy required monarchist leadership in order successfully to represent German interest, I simply do not know what is left to say after the loss of two world wars and the constant decline of German power and welfare. It is hard to see how Germany could have fared worse under a popular government than she did under William II, Tirpitz, Ludendorff, and Hitler. In all probability, Germany on the whole would have had greater strength and less internal dissension; she would have been more in accord with her own European past and have enjoyed greater harmony among her social classes. Again, it was Bismarck who in public speeches always repeated his incitement to the Germans to make a stand against Europe and against those fellow citizens he was pleased to brand "enemies of the Empire."

But the Germans could have found greater unity between their cultural and political life than they were able to achieve after 1850. Friedrich Meinecke's distinction between cultural values and political values seems to be still strongly influenced by the theories of those liberals who, in seeking to conceive of the world of politics as the realm of tragic necessity, but of philosophy, ideology, science, and art as the realm of true freedom, endeavored to justify philosophically their resigned renunciation of establishing political liberty, accepting instead German national unity which Bismarck created through sheer power with the aid of the Prussian army. Meinecke is too much the historical realist ever to have understood this opposition as absolute. In his *Weltbürgertum und Nationalstaat,* he felt he could still overcome the contradiction between German cultural and political values. In his *Idee der Staatsräson,* written after the First World War, he threw the tension into bold relief, whereas in his most recent article, cultural values stand far above political values, but in such a way that a certain sympathy still shines over political events.

In Germany under William II, the doctrine of the difference between individual and general, historical and absolute values, found its leading philosophical advocate in Heinrich Rickert. Wilhelm Dilthey, whom not only Germany but also the world is learning to admire as one of the great German thinkers, declared that Rickert was upholding "an indemonstrable and indeed one-sided definition of the meaning and purpose of history." He added, "This is much too amiable and benevolent a conception of human nature, in which the dark instincts of mutual repression and destruction play a very considerable role." Dilthey was convinced that the power of spiritual ideas was proved by their capacity to conquer the totality of life, just as in turn this totality is the expression of the unity of that infinite-finite being, man.

Almost at the same time as Dilthey penned his criticism of Rickert, Hugo von Hofmannsthal wrote his *Briefe des Zurückgekehrten* (Letters on My Return) (1901), in which he cites as the highest wisdom of the formation of personality the simple statement of a Scotsman, "The whole man must move at once." But Hofmannsthal judged, "that is what Germans are not these days. . . . The thoughts in their heads do not fit the thoughts in their hearts, nor the thoughts of their officials the thoughts of their scholars; the façades of their homes do not fit the backstairs, nor their enterprises their temperament, their public their private life. . . ." At the same time, another great German, Theodor Mommsen, made a moving personal confession in his testament, poignantly expressing the destructive conflict between the political and spiritual-moral natures of Germany at the beginning of the new century.

One of the preconditions for the formulation of a new German concept of history and new forms of social and political organization is the recognition of the unity of life. The state is not just power. It has also the task to realize moral objectives. On the other hand, even the loftiest of ideas do not refute the finite and time-bound character of human nature. Human freedom may be greater in the world of ideas than in political and social action, but, if freedom does not prove itself to be a moral force in the hard conflict with the realities of history, does it have more than an abstract philosophical value? Mere idealism in practical action deserves even less praise. Meinecke's statement that no one should "lecture" a tragic hero "for having taken a wrong path, if, filled with the proud sentiment '*In hoc signo vinces,*' he performs deeds which first carry him to the heights of victory and finally plunge him into the abyss," seems to me wholly untenable. For, in my opinion, the essential difference lies in whether he fights under the sign of the cross, the star symbol of the Prussian Guard, or the swastika. Moreover, the memory of what irreparable wounds were inflicted not only on his own people but also on other nations in the course of such events should indeed never be forgotten. The history of the last fifty years will appear to future historians not only as the history of German defeats, but principally as the history of the political collapse of Europe.

It seems to me that a critical historical evaluation of the last hundred and fifty years of German history can contribute significantly not only to the inner freedom and unity of the German people but also to the development of a new general European consciousness which, in the present state of the world, is a practical necessity. At the same time it is an ideal in harmony with some deep yearnings in German history.

THE HISTORY OF IDEAS*

PROBABLY ALMOST everyone attending the annual meetings
of the American Historical Association, and even more this
year's combined North American meeting, will derive en-
couragement from seeing historical scholarship actively represented by such a strong professional corps. As a group it
seems to possess the capacity of knowing most of the events
in six thousand years of human history, while it is devoted
to filling the pages of history that for one reason or another
have so far remained blank. But at the same time many of us
will feel apprehensive about the course of development that
our historical studies have been taking. The programs of our
meetings clearly demonstrate the continuous growth of specialization and, with it, the danger of the fragmentation of
historical scholarship.

In spite of the eminent position that history holds in general
education, historical thought probably does not exercise the
same strong influence on the formation of the philosophy of
life among our intellectual leaders as was true fifty years ago.
The specialization of historiographical interests is at least
partly responsible for this decline. There are some fundamental questions that historians are unable to answer satisfac-

* Mr. Holborn delivered this presidential address at the Royal York
Hotel, Toronto, Canada, December 29, 1967.

torily at present. Among the most important problems I would count the construction of universal history. Ultimately all historical study will have to be related to the understanding of universal history from which it will receive its sense of final direction. The practical value of a clear conception of universal history for a generation witnessing the meeting of all cultures in global interaction is obvious. The general demand for a model of universal history has led the public again and again to give stormy applause to such theories as Oswald Spengler or Arnold Toynbee presented. But they have kindled only straw fires.

The problem of universal history is, however, only the extreme task whose solution is impeded by the specialization of historical scholarship. Twentieth-century historians deal, actually, in their own work only with small slices of universal history, only, as a matter of fact, with small sections of units of history, mostly circumscribed by nations and epochs. To this division according to subject matter, methodological differences may be added as they have come into existence, as, for example, those between political, economic, and intellectual history. But, although few would deny that division of historical studies often assumes excessive forms, its inevitability cannot be seriously questioned. Once historians accepted the principle that true history could only be written from the original contemporary sources, the needed research rose to gigantic proportions, and the division of labor became ineluctable.

The demand for the writing of history from contemporary sources was an expression of the belief that this was the only way to perceive the real past in all its uniqueness and individuality. Many historians and philosophers feel that the historian's characteristic task is exclusively the study of the individual facts of history.[1] If taken literally, this would lead, and has led, to the assumption that history consists of a huge mass of mutually unrelated facts to be established by independent research. Hand in hand with such an assumption goes the opinion that facts exist outside the mind of the observer and consequently can be simply perceived. They do not call for the judgment of the historian, but, on the contrary, they have to be cleansed of all "subjectivity" that he might bring to them.

These theories, which if strictly applied would produce only the dry bones of history, have often been refuted. Here it may be briefly stated that historical facts, which are dead facts, come to life again only in the mind of the historian and are part of a universal development in which we ourselves partake. A historian who writes and lectures, which means he is using words, cannot help placing the individual event into a larger scheme because language renders the particular in generalizing terms. What we admire in great historians, moreover, is their capacity for relating the individual to the universal, whereby they reveal to us its full historical meaning. Yet it remains true that without the knowledge of the huge variety of individual phenomena history cannot be reproduced and evaluated. But while even the small units reflect something of the totality of human history, through the compartmentalization of historical studies, the historian's vision stays considerably narrowed.

We ought to inquire whether there are approaches to history that can extend our view. The history of ideas or intellectual history, which came into existence relatively late and has gained a place in the American academic curriculum only during the last thirty years, has aroused great expectations, and some of its practitioners even today impress me as being convinced they possess a special key to the inner workings of the historical process. Yet the history of ideas has not achieved a clear and generally accepted definition.

Voltaire was the first, in his *Essai sur les moeurs,* to declare the history of the human mind to be the historian's real subject. Political history is only the tale of external change, whereas in religion, philosophy, science, and art the human mind passes through various stages toward its present state.

Voltaire did not deny that politics had an important part in the rise of human culture; international pacification and the establishment of a firm legal order within a country were for him the foundations of flourishing civilizations. But the rise of the individual to higher self-realization according to his rational nature constituted the true contents of history. Voltaire was not able to make his conception of history prevail for long. He believed that man had remained essentially the same throughout history and that only custom, prejudice, and outward circumstances had hidden and obstructed the power of reason. This belief created a paradox. As Ernst Cassirer expressed it, if the substance of the human mind is immutable, it has no real history.[2]

Hegel followed to some extent in Voltaire's footsteps, while at the same time going far beyond and away from him. The idea of progress was also to Hegel a natural concept in looking at history, and spirit was its real life. But spirit in Hegel's philosophy of history was something quite different from Voltaire's *esprit*. To Hegel history is the unfolding of the universal mind in this world. It occurs when man has risen beyond the state of nature and has begun to use his human potential—thought and reason—which gives him the power to change reality. The rational character of man realizes itself only in the community of men. The state, Hegel says, is the embodiment of morality and links the individual with the great historical development of history. In the state the "objective mind" comes to life. The forms of the state reflect the stage of awareness that man has achieved of the power of reason or of his own freedom. For the "essence of mind is freedom," the freedom that derives from knowing the world as its property.[3]

Hegel strongly emphasizes—perhaps more so than many modern historians—that man is also part of nature and that human passions and appetites are the great incentives of action. But behind the cravings and the struggles of the individuals whose consciousness is impaired by their personal passions, the universal mind moves forward to higher levels. Even the "world-historic" persons, such as Alexander, Caesar, or Napoleon, were driven in their actions by personal interests, but they lived at a moment of history when the existing system of values, laws, and rights was ready to yield to the realization of as yet unfulfilled potentialities; by overthrowing the existing order these great men helped to create a new age. They were not the real initiators of progress but only the agents of the world mind. Hegel speaks of this condition as the "cunning of reason."

Thus history is dominated by the world mind. Though building the world of the objective mind, man is only a laboring puppet. Yet he gains greater freedom as he becomes conscious of the freedom toward which the course of history is directed. Religion, art, and science—for Hegel this meant philosophy—surpass the state. They are forms not of the "objective" but of the "absolute mind," and they enable the individual to know his connection with the universal mind. The dynamic power behind the phenomenal world, however, is still reason, which determines the development of history in accordance with its own laws, the laws of logic. Here, then, Hegel introduces dialectics, the famous sequence of thesis, antithesis, and synthesis.

Only a few of Hegel's key ideas have been sketched here in order to demonstrate that in his view history is a universal process in which each stage has to be judged as an integral part of the whole. But since the really historic is only what is rational, the panlogism of Hegel's philosophy makes ideas the chief objects of historical study. They are the essential achievements of mankind, while at the same time they demarcate the consecutive epochs of history. Hegelian philosophy was for this reason stimulating to the writing of the history of ideas on a large scale. The Tübingen school of Ferdinand Christian Baur applied Hegelian principles to the study of Christian religion, and one of the members of the school, Eduard Zeller, with his book on *The History of Greek Phi-*

losophy[4]—that was considered important and useful enough to justify in recent years a new American edition—carried Hegelian concepts into the history of philosophy. Hegelian influence can still be traced in the modern history of ideas or, for that matter, in general historiography, perhaps most clearly shown in the circumscription of the epochs of history.

But the appeal of Hegel's system faded quickly after his death. In Germany the so-called "Historical School" and Ranke constructed a history in which, to Ranke, "every epoch was equally close to God." This did not allow one to impose on history an a priori pattern or to see in history the fore-ordained course of reason. In contrast to Hegel's monism, Ranke believed in a transcendental God, although he thought that occasionally the historian might discover God's hand in historical events. At the same time, Ranke embraced the totality of human life, including much of what Hegel called "fortuitous existence" (*faule Existenz*), as the true subject of history. And he was anxious by inductive method not only to reconstruct the mere events but to elucidate their meaning in a universal development. The often quoted remark from the foreword to his first work, that he "only wanted to show what actually happened," is bound to be misunderstood if taken out of context. The statement was merely a denial of the intention to present lessons from the past for the present. Although it is true that Ranke in the fifty-odd volumes of his writings concentrated largely on political history, much is found in them on social history as well, particularly in his *English History*, and the author of the *Roman Popes* and of the *German History in the Age of the Reformation* always had an eye on religion.[5]

In Western Europe, Auguste Comte, Herbert Spencer, John Stuart Mill, and others elaborated the "positivistic" philosophy, which was an even more direct continuation of the thought of the Enlightenment than the Hegelian philosophy had been. What Positivism eventually amounted to was the assumption that facts could be immediately ascertained by sense impression and that historical laws could be formulated inductively analogous to the laws of the natural sciences, of which progress remained the most important one. Positivism appeared in many different forms. It did not, in general, emphasize ideas as strongly as Hegel or even Ranke had done; it attempted to counterbalance the study of the individual by the examination of the group and society. After the middle of the nineteenth century, positivism also exercised great influence in Germany, although the German historians, at least in theory, rejected the idea of progress as well as sociology. Hegel and any metaphysical philosophy of history were, on the other hand, declared to be unscientific, and Ranke's students quickly forgot the universalistic ideas of their teacher.

It was in the 1860s that Wilhelm Dilthey began his work as a philosopher and historian. More than any other scholar he was the father of the modern history of ideas. It was a philosophical interest that led Dilthey to history. He objected to the subordination of the humane studies or cultural sciences to the natural sciences, as was common among the Positivists. Even Immanuel Kant had based his theory of knowledge on physics and had not given history and the humanities any recognition as sciences. Dilthey intended to set beside Kant's *Critique of Pure Reason* a *Critique of Historical Reason,* designed to establish the cultural sciences on a secure, scientific basis.

But in contrast to the contemporary German academic philosophers, many of whom attempted to revive Kant, Dilthey felt that philosophy had to part with "logism," the belief that, above the reality, eternal regulating principles exist. In "the spirit of the great Enlightenment," he always intended to retain "the empirical reality as the one world of our knowledge";[6] in this respect he also never denied a kinship with the positivists. Dilthey maintained that philosophy could not go back beyond life. "Life is prior to knowledge."[7] But there is a world of the spirit, which man creates in time through his feeling, willing, and thinking. Man tends to organize his general understanding of what appears to him as his world in a *Weltbild,* that is, world picture, and his own reaction to what the world ought to be or to become in a *Weltanschauung,* or world view. World pictures and world views are the chief sources of our knowledge of the human mind. They are the product of the "living experience" (*Erlebnis*), which we are able to re-experience by an act of empathetic intuition.

For Dilthey the study of the history of ideas was the way to achieve a valid philosophy. It is important that his concept of mind is much more comprehensive than that of Hegel. While Dilthey, too, sees in philosophy the highest capacity of the human spirit, he assigns to the poet probably an even greater creative role, and beside the poetic vision stands the practical will power that finds expression in the laws of the state and society. Philosophy rests largely on the utterances of human imagination and volition and, by abstraction, lifts them to a higher rational level.

Dilthey was the greatest historian of ideas, and although the modern practitioner of the history of ideas often may not be aware of the fact, his influence in this field has been extraordinary. Dilthey's admirable studies, which fill many volumes of his writings, were, however, written with a philosophical intent. They were to him only building stones with which he planned to erect a new system of philosophy. But, if he wanted to extract a philosophy from life or history, he had to solve a major philosophical problem. He himself defined it once in the following words: "Life is given to us not immediately, but elucidated through the objectivation of thought. If the objective conception of life is not to become dubious by the fact that it passes through the operations of thought, the objective validity of thinking will have to be demonstrated."[8] This goal he never reached in his long life.

Dilthey was a philosopher of stature. Although Ortega y Gasset's statement that he was the "most important philosopher in the second half of the nineteenth century"[9] goes too far, Dilthey's philosophy is not only significant as a parallel to William James' pragmatism and to Henri Bergson but also as adumbrating ideas that affected phenomenology, psychoanalysis, and existentialism. Yet Dilthey did not succeed in completing his philosophical system. His studies of the history of Western thought confronted him with a great variety of mutually incompatible world views. Originally he thought that they could be reduced and unified by psychology, and, when physical psychology failed him, he developed a psychology as a branch of the cultural sciences, the so-called descriptive psychology in contrast to the causalistic psychology. But this did not lead him philosophically much further; nor did his last attempts to formulate a typology of philosophical world views establish a common foundation. Dilthey in his last years occasionally tried to comfort himself by pointing out that the universality of the historical consciousness frees man from the limitations of his station and makes him understand the varieties of world views as expressions of human potentialities, thereby challenging his creativity by raising "the activity of man beyond the limitations of the moment and place."[10]

But obviously philosophy would do better if it provided man with a definite world view and a clear set of values in order to enable him to act in the confidence that in his time and place he was representing universal principles. Dilthey, however, admitted with sorrow that the history of ideas leads to relativism, to the "anarchy of world views."[11]

Yet we are more concerned with Dilthey's history of ideas than with his philosophy,[12] although for a moment we shall eventually have to return to the latter. Dilthey's history of ideas has added a new dimension to historiography by expanding it to include, apart from the rational thoughts, the imaginative visions and the conative efforts of man. Not only conflicting systems of philosophy of a period could now be shown to represent various expressions of a common living experience, but the visions of artists and the motivating ideas of statesmen could also be related to the same experience. The spirit of an age, which Hegel and Western Positivism characterized only with naked ideas, could be described in its many-faceted and dynamic life.

At the same time, the historical characterization gained in precision. Jacob Burckhardt, in his classic work on *The Civilization of the Renaissance in Italy* (1860), had described the outlook of the "firstborn modern man," the Italian of that age, in terms such as "individualism" and "realism." Dilthey, a great admirer of the Swiss historian and sage, took exception to these general categories, which were applicable to other centuries as well. In his own "Conception and Analysis of Man in the 15th and 16th Centuries" Dilthey gave a more exact and objective delineation of the Renaissance mind.[13]

It is true that Dilthey's studies on the history of the human mind centered very largely around philosophy, literature, poetry, and music and that he himself did not deal with the visual arts any more than he touched upon political and social ideas. But these were personal rather than philosophical limitations, and others have rounded out the fields to which Dilthey did not directly contribute. Thus Max Dvořák and many historians of art, such as Erwin Panofsky, applied the methods of the history of ideas to the visual arts, and Friedrich Meinecke did the same for political history.

Historians have become willing to accept the analytical findings of the art historians with regard to the artistic styles of various historical periods as adequate descriptions of periods of general history. The term "The Gothic Age" or the "Age of the Baroque" has frequently been used. This makes sense only if one assumes that the artistic style of an age is the projection of an ideal disposition of historical man that determines his actions and reactions equally in all other departments of life. Does not such a view also presuppose that mind or spirit is the ultimate force behind the whole development of history? I suspect that many historians of ideas assume this to be the case and that they are attracted to the study of ideas because it seems to promise the revelation of the innermost causes of historical development. In this form the expectation is not justified. The history of ideas cannot be isolated to the extent that this was done by Dilthey.

Dilthey, as has been said before, wanted to purge the philosophy of history of the "logism" or intellectualism of the Hegelian type. This meant two things: on the one hand, the removal of metaphysics and the demand not to go beyond life itself; on the other, the inclusion of art and religion in a system of world views that superseded the exclusive emphasis on philosophy and science as in Hegel and Comte. But actually Dilthey did not go the whole way. Life in Dilthey's philosophy was identified exclusively with the living experience of the individuals and individual groups that have formulated religions and philosophic ideas or paradigmatic aesthetic forms. This narrowing down to what appears in the consciousness of creative men is far from a consideration of the totality of life. He himself knew that a great reality exists beyond the inward experience of the individual, but he maintains that it is given to us only in symbols, signs, and so forth.[14]

Dilthey was aware that man is a man among men and that as a social being he is conditioned by the society of which he is a member. In one of his articles in which he describes the historical origins of modern science from ancient Greece and Israel to René Descartes and G. W. von Leibniz, he wrote:

The long Middle Ages . . . beginning with the fourteenth century turned toward their end; in the labor of thinking the individual had won his freedom. At the same time a decisive change of the economic life and the social orders of Europe took place, and this resulted in a total shift of intellectual interests. The work of the bourgeois classes in industry and commerce appeared as an independent force in the midst of the feudal and ecclesiastical orders of life. It directed the mind toward this world. Thinking probed into nature and man. The significance of reality and the autonomous value of family, work, and state were felt and recognized.[15]

Yet, although these sentences clearly state a causal connection between ideas and social and economic facts, Dilthey and most of his successors never attempted to establish specific relations between social developments and particular ideas. Thus the sketchy description of the changing social conditions of an age remained more of a painted backdrop of the stage instead of being used to explain the drama itself. Only indirectly does the social structure of a civilization, for Dilthey, affect the progress of the mind that is realized through the life experience of individuals. As an example we may quote the words with which Dilthey in his brilliant study of "The Eighteenth Century and the Historical World" introduces Voltaire. After outlining the political reasons that gave rise to the great culture of England in that age he says: "Voltaire absorbed this ideal of a powerful but free order of society when he came to England. Yet since he was with every fiber a Frenchman, he clung firmly to the independent value of the culture of his joyful fatherland."[16]

No doubt color, and for that matter historical color, is added to the picture of the evolution of ideas by such methods, but no immediate links are created between the social reality and a system of ideas. Actually, however, world views are always created as answers to practical human needs and not only as abstract syntheses. To be sure, the philosopher— and something similar may be said of the poet or artist— may be interested in a study of past philosophical systems without reference to their concrete origins. He wants to study them as paradigmatic thought models with a view of getting inspiration from them. Behind this is the belief in the existence of what Leibniz called the *philosophia perennis*. To the historian, however, this approach is not adequate.

The historian ought to be cognizant of the nature of ideas. The individual forms a life picture in which his position vis-à-vis his fellow men and society is an integral part. He uses ideas to construct a world view that serves not only his self-understanding but also the determination of his attitude to society, which may be reactionary, conservative, reformist, or revolutionary, and this attitude may change within a changing society or the shift of the social status of the individual. Seldom are these fully conscious choices, and the ideas are rarely original, but usually follow a group pattern. Even the man with novel ideas and visions is hardly above the group because he addresses a public that he tries to persuade or possibly spur into action. We must therefore conclude that social history is the necessary complement to the history of ideas. As Ernst Troeltsch stated, without living up to his own advice:

> The rise and development of such theories cannot be detached from the concrete needs and interests of their contemporary environment. . . . They are intellectual structures that cannot be torn from the practical needs and circumstances that create them. They are therefore justified not only from the point of pure theory but mainly from that of their practical contributions and effects.[17]

It seems doubtful to me whether the philosopher Troeltsch did not go too far in this statement by placing the emphasis exclusively on the effects of ideas. Crane Brinton, too, has perhaps unduly narrowed the scope of the history of ideas by saying that it is interested in "the relations between the ideas of the philosophers, the intellectuals, the thinkers, and the actual way of living of the millions who carry the tasks of civilization."[18] I would still believe that even the study of ideas that had no significant influence can be justified if it illustrates the horizons of thinking in the period of their appearance. There are, moreover, ideas that begin to have an impact very late. Arthur Schopenhauer's chief work, *The World as Will and Idea,* appeared in 1819 and received practically no attention. But after 1850 it began to be eagerly read and had a tremendous effect for the rest of the century.

The history of Schopenhauer's influence cannot be explained in terms of the logical unfolding of ideas. It can be understood only through social history. The German intellectuals of 1820 saw in German idealism, and particularly in Hegel's philosophy, the most satisfactory world view in accordance with their living experiences,[19] whereas the generation that had lost the Revolution of 1848–49 and lived in the dawn of the Industrial Revolution turned to Schopenhauer. On an international level the reception of Søren Kierkegaard is comparable. The philosophy of the Danish thinker, who died in 1855, was revived in Germany after World War I, in England in the 1930s, and in America after World War II.

For the explanation of the continued actuality of truncated systems of thought we have again to take recourse in social history. Leaving Marxism alone, little remained alive of Hegel's system after 1840 except the glorification of the state. Hegel's teaching that there is no secular judge of the conflicts of states and that the decision on which state represents the higher historic principle can ultimately be found only in war appealed strongly to the supporters of the new imperialism. Yet a Heinrich von Treitschke had not forgotten that in Hegel's words the state is the embodiment of morality and that religion, art, and science are forms of the absolute spirit. As a consequence, government by law was to Treitschke as much a natural ideal as the toleration and furtherance of free religion, art, and science. Since Hegelianism has been so often called by German Nazi and anti-Nazi professors as by non-German writers a forerunner of National Socialism, it should be pointed out that there is no ideological bridge between the two.[20] National Socialism was absolutely opposed to any universal principle, to free religion, art, and science, and also to government by law. As a matter of fact, to the Nazis the state was not the highest community but rather the *Volk*, and, of course, theirs was not a philosophy of mind but a biological materialism. Hegel's destruction of the philosophical basis of international law may be named a contributing factor not to National Socialism but to its acceptance and support by members of the traditional academic intelligentsia, and this again cannot be judged to be an event exclusively in the history of ideas.

In insisting on the need for social history in conjunction with the history of ideas I do not suggest that the development of ideas ought to be interpreted economically, least of all in the Marxian sense which requires that ideas be made the mere superstructures of the economically conditioned class conflict. Marxism is not improved as a theory of history if it is deprived of its dialectics and its revolutionary prophecy, as is being done by many American scholars who seem to be satisfied to prove that a man just veils his bourgeois sentiment behind ideas labeled objective notions. This ideological debunking seems to me rather dull sport for a historian.

The fundamental difficulty of Marxism is its inadequate picture of the structure of Western society in the various ages. The three classes—feudal, bourgeois, and proletarian —with which Marx operates, although in his strictly historical writings he uses more refined definitions, barely suffice to explain the social movements of an industrializing or industrial society. They are quite inappropriate to the preindustrial society in which social status is affected by many factors other than property, whether landed or financial. The burgher of the fourteenth to the sixteenth century, for example, is hardly comparable to the bourgeois of the industrial society.

It is true, however, that the work for a livelihood and the desire for a secure life are conscious experiences everyone has, and they are bound to affect every world view. There are, undoubtedly, world views that are nothing but structures for the defense or advancement of particular social interests. But not all world views are that narrow. In using ideas the validity of thought has to be defended, and this requires the proof of its universality and autonomy. Over many centuries we observe in Western civilization the growth, by no means even growth, of rationality. The High Middle Ages exhibited such development. In contrast to the East, the West saw no caesaropapism, and the spiritual principle received protection against the political powers from the Roman Church. The Church also nourished a theology in alliance with philosophy. In the development of the medieval cities, groups of merchants and artisans went outside the feudal system, bent upon organizing and administering their business along more rational lines. About the progress toward greater rationality in modern times, it is not necessary to speak here. With it the capacity for the rational control of human affairs has been growing. This control, however, is precarious and constantly imperiled by passions and interests to which the human mind remains forever tied.

There is a continuous interaction between mind, on the one hand, and interest and passions, on the other. The latter two, desiring power, want to make the spirit their servant in order to objectify themselves in ideas. The mind on its part, in order to realize itself, tries to tame interests and passions and force them to allow for the realization of the potentialities of man. The assertion of abstract notions is of no avail in this struggle. The human mind has to take sides without, however, giving up its freedom, which is its true essence if never fully achieved. As a matter of fact, some of the worst dangers that beset the life of the mind stem from the nature of ideas. They tend to become rigid and strongly resistant to replacement by new ideas more fit to reflect novel conditions. But the human mind, in spite of temporary stagnation and grave reverses, has shown itself a decisive force in building civilizations and thereby has not only survived but also gained in strength.

It is the task of history to recognize man in time. Only through history are we able to transcend the limitations of our own station in time and space and become aware of our full potentialities. But this requires placing man in the midst of his total social environment, from which we shall learn about his civilizing strength and weakness. Aiming at the highest historical truth we shall fortify our courage to be free.

Notes

HISTORY AND THE STUDY OF THE CLASSICS

First published in the *Journal of the History of Ideas*, Vol. XIV, No. 1 (January 1953), pp. 33–50.

1. R. Pfeiffer, *Humanitas Erasmiana*, Studien der Bibliothek Warburg, XXII (Leipzig-Berlin, 1931), 4ff.

2. *Ibid.*

3. Cf. W. Dilthey, "Die Entstehung der Hermeneutik," *Gesammelte Schriften*, V (Leipzig-Berlin, 1924), 317ff.

4. I have dealt with this problem from a slightly different aspect in my articles "History and the Humanities" and "Greek and Modern Concepts of History," *Journal of the History of Ideas*, IX (1948), 65ff.; X (1949), 3ff. Now in this volume, pp. 75–80; 62–74.

5. A. Boeckh, *Encyclopädie und Methodologie der philologischen Wissenschaften*, ed. by E. Bratuschek (Leipzig, 1877), 9. This work is based on the lecture courses on the subject which Boeckh gave twenty-six times between 1809 and 1867.

6. Kant defined philology in a very typical eighteenth-century fashion as "the critical knowledge of books and languages." In English, this usage of the word has continued to the present day. German neohumanism gave philology a new and dignified meaning, perhaps first coined and certainly well illustrated by the philosopher Schelling: "The philologist stands with the artist and philosopher on the highest level, or rather the two combine in him" (1803). I have not the time here to discuss the history of the German concept of philology during the subsequent 150 years. The German use of such a term was called forth by the need for giving the inductive sciences a protection against the deductive construction of the past as represented

by Hegel. Later on "philology" was used more and more as the opposite to history. (Cf. for example W. Jaeger's inaugural lecture in Basel [1914] *"Philologie und Historie," Humanistische Reden und Vorträge,* [Berlin-Leipzig, 1937]). I do not think that the German distinction between philology and history is philosophically tenable.

7. A. Boeckh, *op. cit.,* 297.

8. *Ibid.,* 11. On the same page the statement occurs: "philology—or what is the same, history."

9. U. Von Wilamowitz-Moellendorff, *Geschichte der Philologie* (Leipzig-Berlin, 1921), 1 in A. Gercke and E. Norden, eds., *Einleitung in die Altertumswissenschaft,* Vol. 1.

10. Nietzsche, *Wir Philologen* (1874–75) in *Werke (Taschenausgabe),* Vol. 2.

11. A. Boeckh, *op. cit.,* p. 15.

HISTORY AND THE HUMANITIES

First published in *Journal of the History of Ideas,* Vol. IX, No. 1 (New York, 1948), pp. 65–69.

1. José Ortega y Gassett, *Toward a Philosophy of History* (New York, 1941), p. 217, and *Concord and Liberty* (New York, 1946), p. 148.

THE SCIENCE OF HISTORY

First published in *The Interpretation of History,* ed. with an introduction by Joseph R. Strayer, Princeton University Press (New Jersey, 1943), pp. 61–83.

1. *Collected Works,* Vol. 51–52, p. 497.
2. *Ibid.,* Vol. 53–54, p. 61.
3. *Ibid.,* Vol. 33–34, p. vii.
4. *Ibid.,* Vol. 53–54, p. 162.

WILHELM DILTHEY AND THE CRITIQUE
OF HISTORICAL REASON

First published in *Journal of the History of Ideas,* Vol. XI, No. 1 (New York, 1950), pp. 93–118.

1. Cf. Fritz Kaufmann, *Die Philosophie des Grafen Paul Yorck von Wartenburg* (Halle, 1928).

2. *Der junge Dilthey,* ed. by Clara Misch (Leipzig, 1933), p. V.

3. W. Dilthey, *Gesammelte Schriften* (Leipzig, 1914–36). (Hereafter cited as I, II, etc.)

4. *Leben Schleiermachers* (Berlin, 1870). A second edition, augmented by parts of the projected, but never finished second volume, was published by H. Mulert (Berlin, 1922).

5. *Das Erlebnis und die Dichtung* (Leipzig, 1905; ten more editions have been published). *Von Deutscher Dichtung und Musik* (Leipzig, 1932).

6. *Briefwechsel zwischen Wilhelm Dilthey und dem Grafen Paul Yorck von Wartenburg, 1877–1897,* ed. by Sigrid von der Schulenburg (Halle, 1923). (Hereafter cited as *Dilthey-Yorck Briefswechsel.*)

7. *Der junge Dilthey, 1852–70,* ed. by Clara Misch-Dilthey (Leipzig, 1933). Also *"Briefe Wilhelm Diltheys an Bernhard und Luise Scholz, 1859–64,"* ed. by S. von der Schulenburg, *Sitzungsberichte der Preussischen Akademie der Wissenschaften, Phil.-hist. Klasse* (1933), 416–71. These letters show Dilthey's lively interest in music. Dilthey was a leading member of the philosophical faculty of Breslau University that conferred the honorary degree on Brahms for which the composer expressed his gratitude in the Academic Festival Overture. Other Dilthey letters were published by E. Weniger, *"Briefe Wilhelm Diltheys an Rudolf Haym, 1861–73,"* *Abhandlungen der Preussischen Akademie der Wissenschaften* (1936), *Philosophisch-Historische Klasse,* No. 9.

8. G. Misch, *"Lebensphilosophie und Phänomenologie,"* *Philosophischer Anzeiger,* III (1929), 1–102, IV (1930), 175–324, subsequently published as a book (Leipzig, 1930). Cf. also some smaller articles by the same author, recently brought together in *Vom Lebens- und Gedankenkreis Wilhelm Diltheys* (Frankfurt, 1947).

9. O. F. Bollnow, *Dilthey, Eine Einführung in seine Philosophie* (Leipzig, 1936). The most extensive Dilthey bibliography is contained in H. A. Hodges, *Wilhelm Dilthey, An Introduction* (London, 1944),

161–67. The numerous studies of Dilthey's philosophy in German are rather uneven in value, some of them being partly antiquated by the publication of the *Collected Writings;* other and more recent ones are marred by a Nazi slant. I have found most useful the following: E. Spranger, *Wilhelm Dilthey* (Berlin, 1912). M. Scheler, *"Versuche einer Philosophie des Lebens,"* in *Umsturz der Werte*, II, 135–81 (Leipzig, 1923). J. Wach, *Die Typenlehre Trendelenburgs und ihr Einfluss auf Dilthey* (Tübingen, 1926). A Stein, *Der Begriff des Verstehens bei Dilthey* (Tübingen, 1926). L. Landgrebe, *"Wilhelm Diltheys Theorie der Geisteswissenschaften,"* Jahrbuch für philoso- phische und phänomenologische Forschung* (1928). Fritz Kaufmann, *Geschichtsphilosophie der Gegenwart* (Berlin, 1931). C. Cüppers, *Die erkenntnistheoretischen Grundgedanken Wilhelm Diltheys* (Leipzig, 1933). J. Stenzel, *Dilthey und die deutsche Philosophie der Gegenwart* (Berlin, 1934). D. Bischoff, *Wilhelm Diltheys geschichtliche Lebens- philosophie* (Leipzig, 1935).

10. R. Aron, *Essai sur la Théorie de l'Histoire dans l'Allemagne Con- temporaine, La Philosophie Critique de l'Histoire* (Paris, 1938).

11. Cf. his article on Dilthey in *Concord and Liberty* (New York, 1946).

12. Mexico City, ed. by Prof. Imaz, 8 vols.

13. London, 1946. It should not be forgotten that the author did not complete the manuscript and that it was not designed for publication in it present form.

14. See note 9 *supra*.

15. Henry James, ed., *The Letters of William James* (Boston, 1920), I, 109–11.

16. VI, 293, 303; cf. also VIII, iii. According to a letter from Dilthey to Count Yorck in 1896 Dilthey and James exchanged letters. *Dilthey- Yorck Briefwechsel*, 210.

17. K. Jaspers goes so far as to call American pragmatism a "pre- paratory stage of existentialism." *Die geistige Situation der Zeit* (Leip- zig, 1931), 146.

18. H. L. Friess, "Wilhelm Dilthey," *Journal of Philosophy*, XXVI (1929), 5–25. Also G. A. Morgan, "Wilhelm Dilthey," *Philosophical Review*, XLII (1933), 351–80.

19. I, 123.

20. On the connection between Dilthey and positivism see H. A. Hodges, *op. cit.*, 3ff., 70ff.

21. V, 418.

22. VIII, 231. Cf. also *Dilthey-Yorck Briefwechsel*, 146.

23. V, 3.

24. VIII, 175.

25. It is difficult to translate the German term *"Geisteswissenschaften"* into English. The German translator of J. S. Mill's *Logic*, I. Schick, in 1849 rendered the title of the sixth book, "On the logic of the moral sciences," as *Von der Logik der Geisteswissenschaften oder moralischen Wissenschaften.* The term *Geisteswissenschaften* spread amazingly quickly in Germany. For its general acceptance it was most important that Germany's leading scientist, H. Helmholtz, propagated the concept in his famous Heidelberg speech of 1862, "On the relation between the natural sciences and the totality of the sciences." As the English term "moral sciences" superseded the older concept of "moral philosophy," so *Geisteswissenschaften* was used in Germany to describe more aptly what Hegel's philosophy of *Geist* or the romantic theory of *Volksgeist* had aimed at.

Dilthey had not yet used the new term *Geisteswissenschaften* in his article of 1875, "On the study of the history of the sciences of man, society, and the state" (V, 31). Though he mentioned Mill's *"Logik der Geisteswissenschaften,"* he still preferred the term "moral-political sciences." In 1883 his *Einleitung in die Geisteswissenschaften* conceives of the *Geisteswissenschaften* as "the totality of the sciences which have historico-societal reality as their subject-matter." The book made the term classic in Germany. (Cf. for a full history of the term E. Rothacker, *Logik und Systematik der Geisteswissenschaften* [Munich, 1926] 3–16, in *Handbuch der Philosophie,* ed. A. Bäumler and M. Schröter.) But even in the last years of his life Dilthey was still saying: "When beginning with the eighteenth century the need developed to find a common name for this group of sciences, they were called *sciences morales* or *Geisteswissenschaften* or ultimately *Kulturwissenschaften.* This change of names itself shows that none of them is quite adequate to what is to be defined." (VII, 86.) To translate *"Geisteswissenschaften"* as "humanities" is misleading, since they include the social sciences as well. The translation "human studies," which Hodges used (*op. cit.,* 157), seems inadequate for the same reason. I have chosen the translation "cultural sciences" as the relatively best. The chief objection against this translation is that Dilthey himself emphatically rejected H. Rickert's narrower definition of *Kulturwissenschaften.* However, "culture" is used in America in a broader sense than *Kultur* in Germany, and Dilthey's criticism of Rickert would not apply to "cultural sciences."

26. VII, 86; translated by H. A. Hodges, *op. cit.,* 142.

27. I, XVIII. In different translations in H. A. Hodges, *op. cit.,* 113, and in Ortega y Gasset, *Concord and Liberty,* 155.

28. V, 5; cf. also VII, 332ff.

29. VII, 27, 439.

30. V, LXXIX.

31. VIII, 78f.; cf. also VII, 131f.

32. E. M. W. Tillyard, *The Elizabethan World Picture* (London, 1943).

33. V, 379; cf. also VIII, 168.

34. Cf. his inaugural lecture in Basel, "The Poetic and Philosophical Movement in Germany, 1770–1800," V, 12ff.

35. IV, 200.

36. VIII, 264.

37. VII, 7.

38. VI, 189.

39. IV, 200.

40. *Dilthey-Yorck Briefwechsel*, 247.

41. VII, 7.

42. *Dilthey-Yorck Briefwechsel*, 247 and 71.

43. VI, 317ff.

44. VII, 280.

45. "Inwardly no man learns to know his innermost being; for he measures himself according to his own measure, often too small and, unhappily, often too large. Man knows himself only in man. Only life teaches everyone what he is." Goethe, *Tasso*, II, 3; quoted in O. F. Bollnow, *op. cit.*, 150.

46. VII, 320.

47. VII, 206f.

48. VII, 136.

49. VIII, 79.

50. This has been overlooked by R. G. Collingwood, *The Idea of History*, 172; also by D. Bidney, "The Philosophical Anthropology of Ernst Cassirer and Its Significance in Relation to the History of Anthropological Thought," in *The Philosophy of Ernst Cassirer*, ed. P. A. Schilpp (Evanston, 1949), 488ff.

51. W. Windelband, *Geschichte und Naturwissenschaft* (1894); reprinted in his *Praeludien*, 6th ed. (Tübingen, 1919), II, 136–60.

52. H. Rickert, *Die Grenzen der naturwissenschaftlichen Begriffsbildung* (Freiburg, 1896–1902); *Kulturwissenschaft und Naturwissenschaft* (Freiburg, 1899).

53. Cf. my discussion of the English and German terms "cultural sciences," *Geisteswissenschaften, Kulturwissenschaften*, in note 25 *supra*.

54. VII, 172f.

55. I, 26.

56. VII, 323.

57. On Nietzsche's attitude toward history see Karl Jaspers, *Nietzsche* (Berlin, 1936), 205ff.

58. VI, 528f.; cf. also VIII, 162ff., 198.

59. VII, 192.

60. VII, 72.

61. *Ibid.*

62. VI, 315.

63. *Von deutscher Dichtung und Musik*, 78.

64. VII, 72, 229, 325; VIII, 79, 140.

65. VII, 233.

66. VII, 232.

67. V, 200.

68. VII, 233f.; cf. 73, 237, 255; VI, 319.

69. VII, 233.

70. V, 194.

71. *"Ideen über eine beschreibende und zergliedernde Psychologie,"* V, 139–240.

72. V, 177, 167, LXXI. Cf. note 16 *supra.*

73. First published in Halle (1919), since re-edited in a number of editions. His first work was his *Allgemeine Psychopathologie* (1913).

74. R. G. Collingwood in his chapter on Dilthey failed to see that Dilthey's psychology was not constructed, as he asserts, on "naturalistic principles." Most of his criticism of Dilthey thus becomes pointless. *The Idea of History*, 171–76.

75. Halle, 1927.

76. See in the first place his important article, *"Die Entstehung der Hermeneutik,"* V, 317–38. Cf. also E. Spranger, *"Zur Theorie des Verstehens und zur geisteswissenschaftlichen Psychologie,"* *Festschrift für Joh. Volkelt* (Munich, 1918), 357ff., and J. Wach, *Das Verstehen*, 3 vols. (Tübingen, 1926–33).

77. VII, 84.

78. E. Husserl, *Logische Untersuchungen* (Halle, 1900). On the relation between Husserl and Dilthey see G. Misch, *Lebensphilosophie und Phaenomenologie*, l.c.

79. J. Stenzel, *Dilthey und die deutsche Philosophie der Gegenwart* (Berlin, 1934), 17.

80. *Dilthey-Yorck Briefwechsel*, 52; also VII, 248.

81. For a fuller description see H. A. Hodges, *op. cit.*, 99ff.

82. VIII, 8, 147.

83. VIII, 69.

84. VIII, 222.

85. VII, 101ff.; cf. also I, 94; V, 4, 8f.; XI, 216ff.

86. *Dilthey-Yorck Briefwechsel,* 59f., 113, 167.

87. VII, 99, 104.

88. For a fuller treatment of the history of religion in the nineteenth century, in addition to W. Dilthey's own studies on Baur and Zeller in Vol. IV of his *Collected Works,* see E. Troeltsch, *"Adolf von Harnack und Ferdinand Christian Baur," Festgabe für A. von Harnack zum 70. Geburtstage* (Tübingen, 1921), 282ff. Also my article *"Karl Holl," Deutsche Vierteljahrsschrift für Geistesgeschichte und Literaturwissenschaft,* V (1927), 413–30.

89. These studies revolutionized the history of literature and art in Germany and Austria. I mention here as examples only R. Unger, *Literaturgeschichte als Problemgeschichte* (Berlin, 1924), and Max Dvořák, *Kunstgeschichte als Geistesgeschichte* (Munich, 1924).

90. *"Auffassung und Analyse des Menschen im 15. und 16. Jahrhundert,"* II, 1–89.

91. Cf. among others A. Weber's article on *"Kultursoziologie"* and K. Mannheim's article on *"Wissenssoziologie"* in *Handwörterbuch der Soziologie,* ed. by A. Vierkandt (Stuttgart, 1931). Also K. Mannheim *"Ideologische und soziologische Betrachtung der geistigen Gebilde," Jahrbuch für Soziologie,* II (1926), 424–40.

92. VII, 187.

93. XI, 72.

94. XI, 70–76.

95. *Der junge Dilthey,* 81.

96. VIII, 198.

97. VIII, 76f.

98. VIII, 223; cf. VII, 290, VIII, 271.

THE HISTORY OF IDEAS

First published in the *American Historical Review,* Vol. LXXIII (1968), pp. 683–95.

1. Thus in particular the Neo-Kantian school in Germany; see R. G. Collingwood, *The Idea of History* (Oxford, Eng., 1946), 165ff.

2. Ernst Cassirer, *Die Philosophie der Aufklärung* (Tübingen, 1932), 288ff.

3. G. F. W. Hegel, *The Philosophy of History,* tr. J. Sibree (New York, 1899), p. 17.

4. On Baur and Zeller, see Wilhelm Dilthey, *Gesammelte Schriften,* IV (Leipzig, 1921), pp. 403–50.

5. See Hajo Holborn, "The Science of History," in *The Interpretation of History,* ed. Joseph R. Strayer (Princeton, N.J., 1943), 59ff. Now in this volume, pp. 81–97.

6. Wilhelm Dilthey, *Gesammelte Schriften,* V (Leipzig, 1924), p. 418.

7. *Ibid.,* VIII (Leipzig, 1931), p. 264.

8. *Ibid.,* V, p. 5.

9. José Ortega y Gasset, *Concord and Liberty,* tr. Helene Weyl (New York, 1946), p. 131.

10. Dilthey, *Gesammelte Schriften,* V, p. 338.

11. *Ibid.,* VIII, 198.

12. I have dealt at greater length with Dilthey's philosophy in my article "Dilthey's Critique of Historical Reason," *Journal of the History of Ideas,* XI (January 1950), 93ff. For a full bibliography, the following should be added: Gerhard Masur, "Dilthey and the History of Ideas," *ibid.,* XIII (January 1952), 94ff., and the section on Dilthey in *Prophets of Yesterday* (New York, 1961); in addition, Carlo Antoni, *From History to Sociology* (Detroit, 1959), and Wilhelm Dilthey, *Pattern and Meaning in History,* ed. H. P. Rickman (New York, 1962). Now in this volume, pp. 125–52.

13. Dilthey, *Gesammelte Schriften,* II (Leipzig, 1921), iff.

14. *Ibid.,* VIII, p. 225

15. *Ibid.,* III (Leipzig, 1927), p. 8.

16. *Ibid.,* p. 226.

17. Ernst Troeltsch, *Deutscher Geist und Westeuropa* (Tübingen, 1925), p. 19.

18. Crane Brinton, *Ideas and Men* (New York, 1950), p. 7.

19. See Hajo Holborn, "Der deutsche Idealismus in sozialgeschichtlicher Beleuchtung," *Historische Zeitschrift,* CLXXIV (October 1952), pp. 359–84. Now translated in *Germany and Europe* (Anchor Books, New York, 1971).

20. This thesis has been ably proven by Herbert Marcuse, *Reason and Revolution* (2d ed., New York, 1954).

INDEX